Hands-On Functional Programming in Rust

Build modular and reactive applications with functional
programming techniques in Rust 2018

Andrew Johnson

BIRMINGHAM - MUMBAI

Hands-On Functional Programming in Rust

Commissioning Editor: Richa Tripathi
Acquisition Editor: Karan Sadawana
Content Development Editor: Tiksha Sarang
Technical Editor: Adhithya Haridas
Copy Editor: Safis Editing
Project Coordinator: Prajakta Naik
Proofreader: Safis Editing
Indexer: Rekha Nair
Graphics: Jisha Chirayil
Production Coordinator: Shantanu Zagade

First published: May 2018

Production reference: 1300518

Published by Packt Publishing Ltd.
Livery Place
35 Livery Street
Birmingham
B3 2PB, UK.

ISBN 978-1-78883-935-8

www.packtpub.com

`mapt.io`

Mapt is an online digital library that gives you full access to over 5,000 books and videos, as well as industry leading tools to help you plan your personal development and advance your career. For more information, please visit our website.

Why subscribe?

- Spend less time learning and more time coding with practical eBooks and Videos from over 4,000 industry professionals

- Improve your learning with Skill Plans built especially for you

- Get a free eBook or video every month

- Mapt is fully searchable

- Copy and paste, print, and bookmark content

PacktPub.com

Did you know that Packt offers eBook versions of every book published, with PDF and ePub files available? You can upgrade to the eBook version at `www.PacktPub.com` and as a print book customer, you are entitled to a discount on the eBook copy. Get in touch with us at `service@packtpub.com` for more details.

At `www.PacktPub.com`, you can also read a collection of free technical articles, sign up for a range of free newsletters, and receive exclusive discounts and offers on Packt books and eBooks.

Contributors

About the author

Andrew Johnson is a software developer who has worn many hats. Professionally, he has worked on projects written in C, C++, Java, Python, Ruby, JavaScript, Haskell, OCaml, and now Rust. Most notably, he has worked as an early employee at Topsy Labs (acquired by Apple) and FiscalNote (growing rapidly). Academically, his interests are focused on the intersection between formal language processing (such as programming languages) and existing natural language programming techniques.

About the reviewer

Sebastian Dröge is a free software developer currently working with Centricular Ltd. He has been involved for more than 10 years with the GStreamer project, a cross-platform multimedia framework. He also contributes to various other projects, such as Debian, GNOME, Rust, and WebKit. While finishing his master's degree in computer science, he started working as a contractor on free software and continues to do so to this day.

Packt is searching for authors like you

If you're interested in becoming an author for Packt, please visit `authors.packtpub.com` and apply today. We have worked with thousands of developers and tech professionals, just like you, to help them share their insight with the global tech community. You can make a general application, apply for a specific hot topic that we are recruiting an author for, or submit your own idea.

Table of Contents

Preface

Thanks for your interest in functional programming in Rust. Rust is a very young programming language and is particularly new to the functional programming community. Despite its age, the language provides a wealth of tools that are both practical and sophisticated.

In this book, we will introduce general functional programming principles and how they apply to Rust specifically. Our goal is to provide knowledge and a perspective on Rust that will outlast small changes to language features. The pace of development of Rust is so fast that during the course of writing the book we introduced new features as they became available and relevant. We want to equip the reader to produce code for this fast-moving environment such that they are prepared to best utilize new features as they are released.

Who this book is for

This book is for developers who are familiar with basic Rust features or are willing to reference other material as they read along. We will not fully explain every new symbol, library, or syntax form, but we do explain libraries that are considered more advanced or syntax that may be difficult to read. Similarly, some concepts that are only briefly explained in the introductory material will be explained in detail.

What this book covers

Chapter 1, *Functional Programming – a Comparison*, introduces functional programming in Rust. Comparisons are drawn between functional style and other paradigms that are prevalent or influential to Rust. The chapter also serves as a brief outline of topics that will appear later in the book.

Chapter 2, *Functional Control Flow*, introduces Rust control flow structures while explaining how they are relevant to the functional style of programming. The expression-centric nature of functional programming and Rust is illustrated through examples. Limiting as it may be, the chapter also begins an ongoing project using only the procedural expression style of programming.

Chapter 3, *Functional Data Structures*, introduces the reader to the various, highly expressive data types available in Rust. Notably, the enum type is introduced, which holds particular significance in functional programming. The project continues to grow to incorporate a variety of these data types.

Chapter 4, *Generics and Polymorphism*, explains the concepts of parameterization of data (generics) and parameterization of control flow (polymorphism). Parameterization and its natural interaction with traits reduces the programmer's burden, but the syntax can become overwhelming. Some approaches to reduce or mitigate parameter explosion are introduced. The ongoing project again grows to incorporate these features.

Chapter 5, *Code Organization and Application Architecture*, talks about some architectural concerns, recommendations, and best practices. Designing and managing the implementation of a software project is not formulaic. No project is the same, and few are highly similar, thus no engineering procedure can capture the nuances of software development. In this chapter, we provide the best tools available, and specifically, the best that functional programming has to offer.

Chapter 6, *Mutability, Ownership, and Pure Functions*, digs into some of the more unique features in Rust. This chapter introduces the concepts of ownership and lifetimes, which are common stumbling blocks when learning Rust. The functional concepts of immutability and pure functions are also introduced to help untangle some of the spaghetti that a naive Rust programmer might generate when attempting to circumvent the rules of ownership in Rust.

Chapter 7, *Design Patterns*, lists as many functional programming cheat codes that can fit into a single chapter. The concept of functors and monads are explained with examples and some casual definitions. The chapter also briefly introduces the style of functional reactive programming and uses it to build a quick and dirty web framework.

Chapter 8, *Implementing Concurrency*, explains how to do multiple things at the same time. Most of the chapter is spent clarifying the differences and relative strengths and weaknesses between subprocesses, forked processes, and threads. The Rust thread concurrency model is then assumed and more information is provided to clarify Rust-specific logic regarding threads. Toward the end of the chapter, the actor model of concurrency is introduced, which is a robust model of concurrency that can adapt to most situations and programming paradigms.

Chapter 9, *Performance, Debugging, and Metaprogramming,* wraps up the book with some miscellaneous tips for programming in Rust. The performance tips are not particularly functional, but rather concerned primarily with language-specific details, general advice, or relevant bits of computer science. Debugging introduces many tips on how to prevent bugs. Also, how to use an interactive debugger is explained through examples. Metaprogramming explains precisely how Rust macros and procedural macros work. This is a great feature of Rust, but is not documented well, so it might be scary to approach.

To get the most out of this book

1. We assume familiarity with the concepts from the first 10 chapters of Rust documentation (https://doc.rust-lang.org/book/). Some of the material from these chapters is fairly advanced, so we will also explain that here when relevant. However, the knowledge of syntax and very basic features will be expected.
2. Clone the GitHub code repository and follow along. Tweak the examples and see what effects you can create.
3. Stay curious. Some of the keywords we mentioned could fill an entire book with unique content. Some of these topics presented are so pervasive that they have decent Wikipedia articles to explain and expand on the concepts. However, knowing the keyword is required to even know what to search for.

Download the example code files

You can download the example code files for this book from your account at www.packtpub.com. If you purchased this book elsewhere, you can visit www.packtpub.com/support and register to have the files emailed directly to you.

You can download the code files by following these steps:

1. Log in or register at www.packtpub.com.
2. Select the **SUPPORT** tab.
3. Click on **Code Downloads & Errata**.
4. Enter the name of the book in the **Search** box and follow the onscreen instructions.

Once the file is downloaded, please make sure that you unzip or extract the folder using the latest version of:

- WinRAR/7-Zip for Windows
- Zipeg/iZip/UnRarX for Mac
- 7-Zip/PeaZip for Linux

The code bundle for the book is also hosted on GitHub at `https://github.com/PacktPublishing/Hands-On-Functional-Programming-in-Rust`. In case there's an update to the code, it will be updated on the existing GitHub repository.

We also have other code bundles from our rich catalog of books and videos available at `https://github.com/PacktPublishing/`. Check them out!

Conventions used

There are a number of text conventions used throughout this book.

`CodeInText`: Indicates code words in text, database table names, folder names, filenames, file extensions, pathnames, dummy URLs, user input, and Twitter handles. Here is an example: "Let's start by defining some of the type declarations for the `physics` module."

A block of code is set as follows:

```
pub trait MotorController
{
    fn init(&mut self, esp: ElevatorSpecification, est: ElevatorState);
    fn poll(&mut self, est: ElevatorState, dst: u64) -> MotorInput;
}
```

Any command-line input or output is written as follows:

```
closure may outlive the current function, but it borrows `a`, which is
owned by the current function
```

Bold: Indicates a new term, an important word, or words that you see onscreen.

 Warnings or important notes appear like this.

Tips and tricks appear like this.

Get in touch

Feedback from our readers is always welcome.

General feedback: Email `feedback@packtpub.com` and mention the book title in the subject of your message. If you have questions about any aspect of this book, please email us at `questions@packtpub.com`.

Errata: Although we have taken every care to ensure the accuracy of our content, mistakes do happen. If you have found a mistake in this book, we would be grateful if you would report this to us. Please visit `www.packtpub.com/submit-errata`, selecting your book, clicking on the Errata Submission Form link, and entering the details.

Piracy: If you come across any illegal copies of our works in any form on the Internet, we would be grateful if you would provide us with the location address or website name. Please contact us at `copyright@packtpub.com` with a link to the material.

If you are interested in becoming an author: If there is a topic that you have expertise in and you are interested in either writing or contributing to a book, please visit `authors.packtpub.com`.

Reviews

Please leave a review. Once you have read and used this book, why not leave a review on the site that you purchased it from? Potential readers can then see and use your unbiased opinion to make purchase decisions, we at Packt can understand what you think about our products, and our authors can see your feedback on their book. Thank you!

For more information about Packt, please visit `packtpub.com`.

Functional Programming – a Comparison

1

Functional programming (**FP**) is the second most popular programming paradigm, behind only **object-oriented programming** (**OOP**). For many years, these two paradigms have been separated into different languages, so as not to be mixed. Multi-paradigm languages have attempted to support both approaches. Rust is one such language.

As a broad definition, functional programming emphasizes the use of composable and maximally reusable functions to define program behavior. Using these techniques, we will show how functional programming has adapted clever solutions to many common yet difficult problems. This chapter will outline most of the concepts presented in this book. The remaining chapters will be dedicated to helping you master each technique.

The learning outcomes we hope to provide are as follows:

- Being able to use functional style to reduce code weight and complexity
- Being able to write robust safe code by utilizing safe abstractions
- Being able to engineer complex projects using functional principles

Technical requirements

A recent version of Rust is necessary to run the examples provided, and can be found here:

```
https://www.rust-lang.org/en-US/install.html
```

This chapter's code is also available on GitHub, here:

```
https://github.com/PacktPublishing/Hands-On-Functional-Programming-in-RUST
```

Specific installation and build instructions are also included in each chapter's README.md file.

Reducing code weight and complexity

Functional programming can greatly reduce the amount and complexity of code required to accomplish tasks. Particularly in Rust, proper application of functional principles may simplify the often complex design requirements, and make programming a much more productive and rewarding experience.

Making generics more generic

Making generics more generic relates to the practice of parameterizing data structures and functions originated in functional languages. In Rust, and other languages, this is called **generics**. Types and functions can all be parameterized. One or more constraints may be placed on generic types to indicate requirements of a trait or lifetime.

Struct definitions can become redundant without generics. Here is a definition of three structs that define a common concept of a Point. However, the structs use different numerical types, so the singular concept is expanded into three separate PointN type definitions in intro_generics.rs:

```
struct PointU32
{
    x: u32,
    y: u32
}

struct PointF32
{
    x: f32,
    y: f32
}

struct PointI32
{
    x: i32,
    y: i32
}
```

Instead, we can use generics to remove duplicate code and make the code more robust. Generic code is more easily adaptable to new requirements because many behaviors (and thus requirements) can be parameterized. If a change is needed, it is better to only change one line rather than a hundred.

This code snippet defines a parameterized `Point` struct. Now, a single definition can capture all possible numerical types for a `Point` in `intro_generics.rs`:

```
struct Point<T>
{
    x: T,
    y: T
}
```

Functions are also problematic without generics.

Here is a simple function to square a number. However, to capture possible numerical types, we define three different functions in `intro_generics.rs`:

```
fn foo_u32(x: u32) -> u32
{
    x*x
}

fn foo_f32(x: f32) -> f32
{
    x*x
}

fn foo_i32(x: i32) -> i32
{
    x*x
}
```

Function parameters, such as this one, may need trait bounds (a constraint specifying one or more traits) to permit any behavior on that type that is used in the function body.

Here is the `foo` function, redefined with a parameterized type. A single function can define the operation for all numerical types. Explicit bounds must be set for even basic operations, such as multiply or even copy, in `intro_generics.rs`:

```
fn foo<T>(x: T) -> T
where T: std::ops::Mul<Output=T> + Copy
{
    x*x
}
```

Even functions can be sent as parameters. We call these higher-order functions.

Here is a trivial function that accepts a function and argument, then calls the function with the argument, returning the result. Note the trait bound `Fn`, indicating that the provided function is a closure. For an object to be callable, it must implement one of the `fn`, `Fn`, `FnMut`, or `FnOnce` traits in `intro_generics.rs`:

```
fn bar<F,T>(f: F, x: T) -> T
where F: Fn(T) -> T
{
    f(x)
}
```

Functions as values

Functions are nominally the big feature of functional programming. Specifically, functions as values are the keystone of the whole paradigm. Glossing over much detail, we will also introduce the term **closure** here for future reference. A closure is an object that acts as a function, implementing `fn`, `Fn`, `FnMut`, or `FnOnce`.

Simple closures can be defined with the built-in closure syntax. This syntax is also beneficial because the `fn`, `Fn`, `FnMut`, and `FnOnce` traits are automatically implemented if permitted. This syntax is great for shorthand manipulation of data.

Here is an iterator over the range 0 to 10, mapped to the squared value. The square operation is applied using an inline closure definition sent to the `map` function of the iterator. The result of this expression will be an iterator. Here is an expression in `intro_functions.rs`:

```
(0..10).map(|x| x*x);
```

Closures can also have complex bodies with statements if the block syntax is used.

Here is an iterator from 0 to 10, mapped with a complex equation. The closure provided to map includes a function definition and a variable binding in `intro_functions.rs`:

```
(0..10).map(|x| {
    fn f(y: u32) -> u32 {
        y*y
    }
    let z = f(x+1) * f(x+2);
    z*z
}
```

It is possible to define functions or methods that accept closures as arguments. To use the closure as a callable function, a bound of `Fn`, `FnMut`, or `FnOnce` must be specified.

Here is a HoF definition accepting a function g and an argument x. The definition constrains g and x to process `u32` types, and defines some mathematical operations involving calls to g. An invocation of the f HoF is also provided, as follows, using a simple inline closure definition in `intro_functions.rs`:

```
fn f<T>(g: T, x: u32) -> u32
where T: Fn(u32) -> u32
{
    g(x+1) * g(x+2)
}

fn main()
{
    f(|x|{ x*x }, 2);
}
```

Many parts of the standard library, particularly iterators, encourage heavy use of functions as arguments.

Here is an iterator from 0 to 10 followed by many chained iterator combinators. The map function returns a new value from an original. `inspect` looks at a value, does not change it, but permits side-effects. `filter` omits all values that do not satisfy a predicate. `filter_map` filters and maps with a single function. The `fold` reduces all results to a single value, starting from an initial value, working left to right. Here is the expression in `intro_functions.rs`:

```
(0..10).map(|x| x*x)
       .inspect(|x|{ println!("value {}", *x) })
       .filter(|x| *x<3)
       .filter_map(|x| Some(x))
       .fold(0, |x,y| x+y);
```

Iterators

Iterators are a common feature of OOP languages, and Rust supports this concept well. Rust iterators are also designed with functional programming in mind, allowing programmers to write more legible code. The specific concept emphasized here is **composability**. When iterators can be manipulated, transformed, and combined, the mess of `for` loops can be replaced by individual function calls. These examples can be found in the `intro_iterators.rs` file. This is depicted in the following table:

Function name with description	Example
Chain concatenates two iterators: `first...second`	`(0..10).chain(10..20);`
The `zip` function combines two iterators into tuple pairs, iterating until the end of the shortest iterator: (a1,b1), (a2, b2), ...	`(0..10).zip(10..20);`
The `enumerate` function is a special case of `zip` that creates numbered tuples (0, a1),(1,a2), ...	`(0..10).enumerate();`
The `inspect` function applies a function to all values in the iterator during iteration	`(0..10).inspect(|x|{ println!("value {}", *x) });`
The `map` function applies a function to each element, returning the result in place	`(0..10).map(|x| x*x);`
The `filter` function restricts elements to those satisfying a predicate	`(0..10).filter(|x| *x<3);`
The `fold` function accumulates all values into a single result	`(0..10).fold(0, |x,y| x+y);`

When you want to apply the iterator, you can use a `for` loop or call `collect`	`for i in (0..10) {}`
	
	`(0..10).collect::<Vec<u64>>();`

Compact legible expressions

In functional languages, all terms are expressions. There are no statements in function bodies, only a single expression. All control flow operators are then formulated as expressions with a return value. In Rust, this is almost the case; the only non-expressions are `let` statements and item declarations.

Both of these statements can be wrapped in blocks to create an expression along with any other term. An example for this is the following, in `intro_expressions.rs`:

```
let x = {
    fn f(x: u32) -> u32 {
        x * x
    }
    let y = f(5);
    y * 3
};
```

This nested format is uncommon in the wild, but it illustrates the permissive nature of Rust grammar.

Returning to the concept of functional style expressions, the emphasis should always be on writing legible literate code without much hassle or bloat. When someone else, or you at a later time, comes to read your code, it should be immediately understandable. Ideally, the code should document itself. If you find yourself constantly writing code twice, once in code and again as comments, then you should reconsider how effective your programming practices really are.

To start with some examples of functional expressions, let's look at an expression that exists in most languages, the ternary conditional operator. In a normal `if` statement, the condition must occupy its own line and thus cannot be used as a sub-expression.

The following is a traditional `if` statement, initializing a variable in `intro_expressions.rs`:

```
let x;
if true {
    x = 1;
} else {
    x = 2;
}
```

With the ternary operator, this assignment can be moved to a single line, shown as follows in `intro_expressions.rs`:

```
let x = if true { 1 } else { 2 };
```

Almost every statement from OOP in Rust is also an expression—if, for, while, and so on. One of the more unique expressions to see in Rust that is uncommon in OOP languages is direct constructor expressions. All Rust types can be instantiated by single expressions. Constructors are only necessary in specific cases, for example, when an internal field requires complex initialization. The following is a simple struct and an equivalent tuple in intro_expressions.rs:

```rust
struct MyStruct
{
    a: u32,
    b: f32,
    c: String
}

fn main()
{
    MyStruct {
        a: 1,
        b: 1.0,
        c: "".to_string()
    };

    (1, 1.0, "".to_string());
}
```

Another distinctive expression from functional languages is pattern matching. Pattern matching can be thought of as a more powerful version of a switch statement. Any expression can be sent into a pattern expression and de-structured to bind internal information into local variables before executing a branch expression. Pattern expressions are uniquely suited for working with enums. The two make a perfect pair.

The following snippet defines a Term as a tagged union of expression options. In the main function, a Term t is constructed, then matched with a pattern expression. Note the syntax similarity between the definition of a tagged union and the matching inside of a pattern expression in intro_expressions.rs:

```rust
enum Term
{
    TermVal { value: String },
    TermVar { symbol: String },
    TermApp { f: Box<Term>, x: Box<Term> },
    TermAbs { arg: String, body: Box<Term> }
}

fn main()
```

```
{
    let mut t = Term::TermVar {
        symbol: "".to_string()
    };
    match t {
        Term::TermVal { value: v1 } => v1,
        Term::TermVar { symbol: v1 } => v1,
        Term::TermApp { f: ref v1, x: ref v2 } =>
            "TermApp(?,?)".to_string(),
        Term::TermAbs { arg: ref mut v1, body: ref mut v2 } =>
            "TermAbs(?,?)".to_string()
    };
}
```

Strict abstraction means safe abstraction

Having a stricter type system does not imply that code will have more requirements or be any more complex. Rather than strict typing, consider using the term expressive typing. Expressive typing provides more information to the compiler. This extra information allows the compiler to provide extra assistance while programming. This extra information also permits a very rich metaprogramming system. This is all in addition to the obvious benefit of safer, more robust code.

Scoped data binding

Variables in Rust are treated much more strictly than in most other languages. Global variables are almost entirely disallowed. Local variables are put under close watch to ensure that allocated data structures are properly deconstructed before going out of scope, but not sooner. This concept of tracking a variable's proper scope is known as **ownership** and **lifetime**.

In a simple example, data structures that allocate memory will deconstruct automatically when they go out of scope. No manual memory management is required in `intro_binding.rs`:

```
fn scoped() {
    vec![1, 2, 3];
}
```

In a slightly more complex example, allocated data structures can be passed around as return values, or referenced, and so on. These exceptions to simple scoping must also be accounted for in `intro_binding.rs`:

```
fn scoped2() -> Vec<u32>
{
    vec![1, 2, 3]
}
```

This usage tracking can get complicated (and undecidable), so Rust has some rules that restrict when a variable can escape a context. We call this **complex rules ownership**. It can be explained with the following code, in `intro_binding.rs`:

```
fn scoped3()
{
    let v1 = vec![1, 2, 3];
    let v2 = v1;
    //it is now illegal to reference v1
    //ownership has been transferred to v2
}
```

When it is not possible or desirable to transfer ownership, the `clone` trait is encouraged to create a duplicate copy of whatever data is referenced in `intro_binding.rs`:

```
fn scoped4()
{
    vec![1, 2, 3].clone();
    "".to_string().clone();
}
```

Cloning or copying is not a perfect solution, and comes with a performance overhead. To make Rust faster, and it is pretty fast, we also have the concept of borrowing. Borrowing is a mechanism to receive a direct reference to some data with the promise that ownership will be returned by some specific point. References are indicated by an ampersand. Consider the following example, in `intro_binding.rs`:

```
fn scoped5()
{
    fn foo(v1: &Vec<u32>)
    {
        for v in v1
        {
            println!("{}", v);
        }
    }
```

```
let v1 = vec![1, 2, 3];
foo(&v1);

//v1 is still valid
//ownership has been returned
v1;
}
```

Another benefit of strict ownership is safe concurrency. Each binding is owned by a particular thread, and that ownership can be transferred to new threads with the move keyword. This has been explained with the following code, in intro_binding.rs:

```
use std::thread;

fn thread1()
{
    let v = vec![1, 2, 3];

    let handle = thread::spawn(move || {
        println!("Here's a vector: {:?}", v);
    });

    handle.join().ok();
}
```

To share information between threads, programmers have two main options.

First, programmers may use the traditional combination of locks and atomic references. This is explained with the following code, in intro_binding.rs:

```
use std::sync::{Mutex, Arc};
use std::thread;

fn thread2()
{

    let counter = Arc::new(Mutex::new(0));
    let mut handles = vec![];

    for _ in 0..10 {
        let counter = Arc::clone(&counter);
        let handle = thread::spawn(move || {
            let mut num = counter.lock().unwrap();
            *num += 1;
        });
        handles.push(handle);
    }
```

```
      for handle in handles {
         handle.join().unwrap();
      }

      println!("Result: {}", *counter.lock().unwrap());
   }
```

Second, channels provide a nice mechanism for message passing and job queuing between threads. The send trait is also implemented automatically for most objects. Consider the following code, in intro_binding.rs:

```
use std::thread;
use std::sync::mpsc::channel;

fn thread3() {

   let (sender, receiver) = channel();
   let handle = thread::spawn(move ||{

      //do work
      let v = vec![1, 2, 3];
      sender.send(v).unwrap();

   });

   handle.join().ok();
   receiver.recv().unwrap();
}
```

All of this concurrency is type-safe and compiler-enforced. Use threads as much as you want, and if you accidentally try to create a race condition or simple deadlock, then the compiler will stop you. We call this **fearless concurrency**.

Algebraic datatypes

In addition to structs/objects and functions/methods, Rust functional programming includes some rich additions to definable types and structures. Tuples provide a shorthand for defining simple anonymous structs. Enums provide a type-safe approach to unions of complex data structures with the added bonus of a constructor tag to help in pattern matching. The standard library has extensive support for generic programming, from base types to collections. Even the object system traits are a hybrid cross between the OOP concept of a class and the FP concept of type classes. Functional style lurks around every corner, and even if you don't seek them in Rust, you will probably find yourself unknowingly using the features.

The `type` aliases can be helpful to create shorthand names for complex types. Alternatively, the `newtype` struct pattern can be used to create an alias with different non-equivalent types. Consider the following example, in `intro_datatypes.rs`:

```
//alias
type Name = String;

//newtype
struct NewName(String);
```

A `struct`, even when parameterized, can be repetitive when used simply to store multiple values into a single object. This can be seen in `intro_datatypes.rs`:

```
struct Data1
{
    a: i32,
    b: f64,
    c: String
}

struct Data2
{
    a: u32,
    b: String,
    c: f64
}
```

A tuple helps eliminate redundant struct definitions. No prior type definitions are necessary to use tuples. Consider the following example, in `intro_datatypes.rs`:

```
//alias to tuples
type Tuple1 = (i32, f64, String);
type Tuple2 = (u32, String, f64);

//named tuples
struct New1(i32, f64, String);
struct New2(u32, String, f64);
```

Standard operators can be implemented for any type by implementing the correct trait. Consider the following example for this, in `intro_datatypes.rs`:

```
use std::ops::Mul;

struct Point
{
    x: i32,
    y: i32
```

```
    }

    impl Mul for Point
    {
        type Output = Point;
        fn mul(self, other: Point) -> Point
        {
            Point
            {
                x: self.x * other.x,
                y: self.y * other.y
            }
        }
    }
```

Standard library collections and many other built-in types are generic, such as `HashMap` in `intro_datatypes.rs`:

```
    use std::collections::HashMap;

    type CustomHashMap = HashMap<i32,u32>;
```

Enums are a type-safe union of multiple types. Note that recursive `enum` definitions must wrap the inner value in a container such as `Box`, otherwise the size would be infinite. This is depicted as follows, in `intro_datatypes.rs`:

```
    enum BTree<T>
    {
        Branch { val:T, left:Box<BTree<T>>, right:Box<BTree<T>> },
        Leaf { val: T }
    }
```

Tagged unions are also used for more complex data structures. Consider the following code, in `intro_datatypes.rs`:

```
    enum Term
    {
        TermVal { value: String },
        TermVar { symbol: String },
        TermApp { f: Box<Term>, x: Box<Term> },
        TermAbs { arg: String, body: Box<Term> }
    }
```

Traits are a bit like object classes (OOP), shown with the following code example, in `intro_datatypes.rs`:

```
trait Data1Trait
{
    //constructors
    fn new(a: i32, b: f64, c: String) -> Self;
    //methods
    fn get_a(&self) -> i32;
    fn get_b(&self) -> f64;
    fn get_c(&self) -> String;
}
```

Traits are also like type classes (FP), shown with the following code snippet, in `intro_datatypes.rs`:

```
trait BehaviorOfShow
{
    fn show(&self) -> String;
}
```

Mixing object-oriented programming and functional programming

As mentioned before, Rust supports much of both object-oriented and functional programming styles. Datatypes and functions are neutral to either paradigm. Traits specifically support a hybrid blend of both styles.

First, in an object-oriented style, defining a simple class with a constructor and some methods can be accomplished with a `struct`, `trait`, and `impl`. This is explained using the following code snippet, in `intro_mixoopfp.rs`:

```
struct MyObject
{
    a: u32,
    b: f32,
    c: String
}

trait MyObjectTrait
{
    fn new(a: u32, b: f32, c: String) -> Self;
    fn get_a(&self) -> u32;
    fn get_b(&self) -> f32;
```

```
        fn get_c(&self) -> String;
}

impl MyObjectTrait for MyObject
{
    fn new(a: u32, b: f32, c: String) -> Self
    {
        MyObject { a:a, b:b, c:c }
    }

    fn get_a(&self) -> u32
    {
        self.a
    }

    fn get_b(&self) -> f32
    {
        self.b
    }

    fn get_c(&self) -> String
    {
        self.c.clone()
    }
}
```

Adding support for functional programming onto an object is as simple as defining traits and methods that use functional language features. For example, accepting a closure can become a great abstraction when used appropriately. Consider the following example, in intro_mixoopfp.rs:

```
trait MyObjectApply
{
    fn apply<F,R>(&self, f:F) -> R
    where F: Fn(u32,f32,String) -> R;
}

impl MyObjectApply for MyObject
{
    fn apply<F,R>(&self, f:F) -> R
    where F: Fn(u32,f32,String) -> R
    {
        f(self.a, self.b, self.c.clone())
    }
}
```

Improving project architecture

Functional programs encourage good project architecture and principled design patterns. Using the building blocks of functional programming often reduces the number of design choices to be made in such a way that good options become obvious.

"There should be one - and preferably only one - obvious way to do it."

– PEP 20

File hierarchy, modules, and namespace design

Rust programs are compiled primarily in one of two ways. The first is to use `rustc` to compile individual files. The second is to describe an entire package for compilation using `cargo`. We will assume here that projects are built using `cargo`, as follows:

1. To start a package, you first create a `Cargo.toml` file in a directory. That directory will be your package directory from now on. This is a configuration file that will tell the compiler what code, assets, and extra information should be included into the package:

```
[package]
name = "fp_rust"
version = "0.0.1"
```

2. After this basic configuration, you can now use `cargo build` to compile the entire project. Where you decide to place your code files, and what to name them, is determined by how you want to refer to them in the module namespace. Each file will be given its own module `mod`. You can also nest modules inside files:

```
mod inner_module
{
    fn f1()
    {
        println!("inner module function");
    }
}
```

3. After these steps, projects can then be added as cargo dependencies, and namespaces can be used inside of modules to expose public symbols. Consider the following code snippet:

```
extern crate package;
use package::inner_module::f1;
```

These are the basic building blocks of Rust modules, but what does this have to do with functional programming?

Architecting a project in functional style is a process, and lends itself to certain routines. Typically, the project architect will start by designing the core data structures and in complex cases also the physical structure (where code/services will operationally be run). Once the data layout has been outlined in sufficient detail, then core functions/routines can be planned (such as how the program behaves). Up to this point, there may be code left unimplemented if coding is happening during the architecting stage. The final stage involves replacing this mock code with correct behaviors.

Following this stage-by-stage development process, we can also see an archetypical file layout forming. It is common to see these stages written top to bottom in actual programs. Though it is unlikely the authors went through planning in these explicit stages, it still is a common pattern due to simplicity's sake. Consider the following example:

```
//trait definitions

//data structure and trait implementations

//functions

//main
```

Grouping definitions like this may be helpful to standardize file layout and improve readability. Searching back and forth through a long file for symbol definitions is a common but unpleasant part of programming. It is also a preventable problem.

Functional design patterns

Aside from file layout, there are a number of functional design patterns that help reduce code weight and redundancy. When used properly, these principles can help clarify design decisions and also enable robust architecture. Most design patterns are variants of the single responsibility principle. This can take many forms depending on the context, but the intent is the same; write code that does one thing well, then reuse that code as needed. I have explained this as follows:

- **Pure functions**: These are functions with no side effects or logical dependencies other than function arguments. A side effect is a change of state that affects anything outside of the function, aside from the return value. Pure functions are useful because they can be tossed around and combined and generally used carelessly without the risk of unintended effects.

 The worst thing that can go wrong with a pure function is a bad return value or, in extreme cases, a stack overflow.

It is harder to cause bugs with pure functions, even when used recklessly. Consider the following example of pure functions, in `intro_patterns.rs`:

```rust
fn pure_function1(x: u32) -> u32
{
    x * x
}

fn impure_function(x: u32) -> u32
{
    println!("x = {}", x);
    x * x
}
```

- **Immutability**: Immutability is a pattern that helps encourage pure functions. Rust variable bindings are immutable by default. This is Rust's not-so-subtle way of encouraging you to avoid mutable state. Don't do it. If you absolutely must, it is possible to tag variables with the `mut` keyword to allow reassignment. This is shown with the following example, in `intro_patterns.rs`:

```
let immutable_v1 = 1;
//immutable_v1 = 2; //invalid

let mut mutable_v2 = 1;
mutable_v2 = 2;
```

- **Functional composition**: Functional composition is a pattern where the output of one function is connected to the input of another function. In this fashion, functions can be chained together to create complex effects from simple steps. This is shown with the following code snippet, in `intro_patterns.rs`:

```
let fsin = |x: f64| x.sin();
let fabs = |x: f64| x.abs();

//feed output of one into the other
let transform = |x: f64| fabs(fsin(x));
```

- **Higher-order functions**: These have already been mentioned before, but we haven't used the term yet. A HoF is a function that accepts a function as a parameter. Many iterator methods are HoFs. Consider the following example, in `intro_patterns.rs`:

```
fn filter<P>(self, predicate: P) -> Filter<Self, P>
where P: FnMut(&Self::Item) -> bool
{ ... }
```

- **Functors**: If you can get past the name, these are a simple and effective design pattern. They are also very versatile. The concept is somewhat difficult to capture in its entirety, but you may think of functors as *the inverse of functions*. A function defines a transformation, accepts data, and returns the result of the transformation. A functor defines data, accepts a function, and returns the result of the transformation. A common example of a functor is the bound `map` method that frequently appears on containers, such as for a `Vec`. Here is an example, in `intro_patterns.rs`:

```
let mut c = 0;
for _ in vec!['a', 'b', 'c'].into_iter()
    .map(|letter| {
        c += 1; (letter, c)
    }){};
```

"A monad is a monoid in the category of endofunctors, what's the problem?"

– *Philip Wadler*

- **Monads**: Monads are a common stumbling block for people learning FP. Monads and functors are maybe the first words that you may encounter on a journey that goes deep into theoretical mathematics. We won't go there. For our purposes, monads are simply a `trait` with two methods. This is shown in the following code, in `intro_patterns.rs`:

```
trait Monad<A> {
    fn return_(t: A) -> Self;
    //:: A -> Monad<A>

    fn bind<MB,B>(m: Self, f: Fn(A) -> MB) -> MB
    where MB: Monad<B>;
    //:: Monad<A> -> (A -> Monad<B>) -> Monad<B>
}
```

If that doesn't help clarify things (and it probably doesn't), a monad has two methods. The first method is the constructor. The second method lets you bind an operation to create another monad. Many common traits have hidden semi-monads but, by making the concept explicit, the concept becomes a strong design pattern instead of a messy anti-pattern. Don't try to reinvent what you don't have to.

- **Function currying**: Function currying is a technique that may seem strange for anyone coming from a background in object-oriented or imperative languages. The reason for this confusion is that in many functional languages, functions are curried by default, whereas this is not the case for other languages. Rust functions are not curried by default.

The difference between curried and non-curried functions are that curried functions send in parameters one by one, whereas non-curried functions send in parameters all at once. Looking at a normal Rust function definition, we can see that it is not curried. Consider the following code, in intro_patterns.rs:

```
fn not_curried(p1: u32, p2: u32) -> u32
{
    p1 + p2
}

fn main()
{
    //and calling it
    not_curried(1, 2);
}
```

A curried function takes each parameter one by one, as shown in the following, in intro_patterns.rs:

```
fn curried(p1: u32) -> Box<Fn(u32) -> u32>
{
    Box::new(move |p2: u32| {
        p1 + p2
    })
}

fn main()
{
    //and calling it
    curried(1)(2);
}
```

Curried functions can be used as a function factory. The first few arguments configure how the final function should behave. The result is a pattern that allows shorthand configuration of complex operators. Currying complements all the other design patterns by converting individual functions into multiple components.

- **Lazy evaluation**: Lazy evaluation is a pattern that is technically possible in other languages. However, it is uncommon to see it outside of FP, due to language barriers. The difference between a normal expression and a lazy expression is that a lazy expression will not be evaluated until accessed. Here is a simple implementation of laziness, implemented behind a function call in intro_patterns.rs:

```
let x = { println!("side effect"); 1 + 2 };

let y = ||{ println!("side effect"); 1 + 2 };
```

The second expression will not be evaluated until the function is called, at which point the code resolves. For lazy expressions, side effects happen at time of resolution instead of at initialization. This is a poor implementation of laziness, so we will go into further detail in later chapters. The pattern is fairly common, and some operators and data structures require laziness to work. A simple example of necessary laziness is a lazy list that may not otherwise be possible to create. The built-in Rust numerical iterator (lazy list) uses this well: (0..).

Memoization is the last pattern that we will introduce here. It may be considered as more of an optimization than design pattern, but due to how common it is, we should mention it here. A memoized function only computes unique results once. A simple implementation would be a function guarded by a hash table. If the parameters and result are already in the hash table, then skip the function call and directly return the result from the hash table. Otherwise, compute the result, put it in the hash table, and return. This process can be implemented manually in any language, but Rust macros allow us to write the memoization code once, and reuse that code by applying this macro. This is shown using the following code snippet, in intro_patterns.rs:

```
#[macro_use] extern crate cached;
#[macro_use] extern crate lazy_static;

cached! {
    FIB;
    fn fib(n: u64) -> u64 = {
        if n==0 || n==1 { return n }
        fib(n-1) + fib(n-2)
    }
}

fn main()
{
    fib(30);
}
```

This example makes use of two crates and many macros. We won't fully explain everything that is happening here until the very end of this book. There is much that is possible with macros and metaprogramming. Caching function results is just a start.

Metaprogramming

The term metaprogramming in Rust often overlaps with the term macros. There are two primary types of macros available in Rust:

- Recursive
- Procedural

Both types of macros take as input an **abstract syntax tree** (**AST**), and produce one or more AST.

A commonly used macro is `println`. A variable number of arguments and types are joined with the format string through the use of a macro to produce formatted output. To invoke recursive macros like this, invoke the macro just like a function with the addition of a `!` before the arguments. Macro applications may alternatively be surrounded by `[]` or `{}`:

```
vec!["this is a macro", 1, 2];
```

Recursive macros are defined by `macro_rules!` statements. The inside of a `macro_rules` definition is very similar to that of a pattern-matching expression. The only difference is that `macro_rules!` matches syntax instead of data. We can use this format to define a reduced version of the `vec` macro. This is shown in the following code snippet, in `intro_metaprogramming.rs`:

```
macro_rules! my_vec_macro
{
    ( $( $x:expr ),* ) =>
    {
        {
            let mut temp_vec = Vec::new();
            $(
                temp_vec.push($x);
            )*
            temp_vec
        }
    }
}
```

This definition accepts and matches only one pattern. It expects a comma-separated list of expressions. The syntax pattern ($($x: expr),*) matches against a comma-separated list of expressions and stores the result in the plural variable $x. In the body of the expression, there is a single block. The block defines a new vec, then iterates through $x* to push each $x into the vec, and, finally, the block returns the vec as its result. The macro and its expansion are as follows, in intro_metaprogramming.rs:

```
//this
my_vec_macro!(1, 2, 3);

//is the same as this
{
    let mut temp_vec = Vec::new();
    temp_vec.push(1);
    temp_vec.push(2);
    temp_vec.push(3);
    temp_vec
}
```

It is important to note that expressions are moved as code, not as values, so side effects will be moved to the evaluating context, not the defining context.

Recursive macro patterns match against token strings. It is possible to execute separate branches depending on which tokens are matched. A simple case match looks like the following, in intro_metaprogramming.rs:

```
macro_rules! my_macro_branch
{
    (1 $e:expr) => (println!("mode 1: {}", $e));
    (2 $e:expr) => (println!("mode 2: {}", $e));
}

fn main()
{
    my_macro_branch!(1 "abc");
    my_macro_branch!(2 "def");
}
```

The name recursive macros comes from recursion in the macros, so of course we can call into the macro that we are defining. Recursive macros could be a quick way to define a domain-specific language. Consider the following code snippet, in intro_metaprogramming.rs:

```
enum DSLTerm {
    TVar { symbol: String },
    TAbs { param: String, body: Box<DSLTerm> },
```

```
        TApp { f: Box<DSLTerm>, x: Box<DSLTerm> }
}

macro_rules! dsl
{
    ( ( $($e:tt)* ) ) => (dsl!( $($e)* ));
    ( $e:ident ) => (DSLTerm::TVar {
        symbol: stringify!($e).to_string()
    });
    ( fn $p:ident . $b:tt ) => (DSLTerm::TAbs {
        param: stringify!($p).to_string(),
        body: Box::new(dsl!($b))
    });
    ( $f:tt $x:tt ) => (DSLTerm::TApp {
        f: Box::new(dsl!($f)),
        x: Box::new(dsl!($x))
    });
}
```

The second form of macro definitions is procedural macros. Recursive macros can be thought of as a nice syntax to help define procedural macros. Procedural macros, on the other hand, are the most general form. There are many things you can do with procedural macros that are simply impossible with the recursive form.

Here, we can grab the `TypeName` of a `struct` and use that to automatically generate a trait implementation. Here is the macro definition, in `intro_metaprogramming.rs`:

```
#![crate_type = "proc-macro"]
extern crate proc_macro;
extern crate syn;
#[macro_use]
extern crate quote;
use proc_macro::TokenStream;
#[proc_macro_derive(TypeName)]

pub fn type_name(input: TokenStream) -> TokenStream
{
    // Parse token stream into input AST
    let ast = syn::parse(input).unwrap();
    // Generate output AST
    impl_typename(&ast).into()
}

fn impl_typename(ast: &syn::DeriveInput) -> quote::Tokens
{
    let name = &ast.ident;
    quote!
```

```
    {
        impl TypeName for #name
        {
            fn typename () -> String
            {
                stringify! (#name).to_string()
            }
        }
    }
}
```

The corresponding macro invocation looks like the following, in
`intro_metaprogramming.rs`:

```
#[macro_use]
extern crate metaderive;

pub trait TypeName
{
    fn typename () -> String;
}

#[derive(TypeName)]
struct MyStructA
{
    a: u32,
    b: f32
}
```

As you can see, procedural macros are a bit more complicated to set up. However, the benefit is then that all processing is done directly with normal Rust code. These macros permit use of any syntactic information in unstructured format to generate more code structures before compilation.

Procedural macros are handled as separate modules to be precompiled and executed during normal compiler execution. The information provided to each macro is localized, so whole program consideration is not possible. However, the available local information is sufficient to achieve some fairly complicated effects.

Summary

In this chapter, we briefly outlined the major concepts that will appear throughout this book. From the code examples, you should now be able to visually identify functional style. We also mentioned some of the reasons why these concepts are useful. In the remaining chapters, we will provide full context to when and why each technique would be appropriate. In that context, we will also provide the knowledge required to master the techniques and start using functional practices.

From this chapter, we learned to parameterize as much as possible, and that functions can be used as parameters, to define complex behavior by combining simple behaviors, and that it is safe to use threads however you want in Rust as long as it compiles.

This book is structured to introduce simpler concepts first, then, as the book continues, some concepts may become more abstract or technical. Also, all techniques will be introduced in the context of an ongoing project. The project will control an elevator system, and the requirements will gradually become more demanding as the book progresses.

Questions

1. What is a function?
2. What is a functor?
3. What is a tuple?
4. What control flow expression was designed for use with tagged unions?
5. What is the name for a function with a function as a parameter?
6. How many times will `fib` be called in memoized `fib(20)`?
7. What datatypes can be sent over a channel?
8. Why do functions need to be boxed when returned from a function?
9. What does the `move` keyword do?
10. How could two variables share ownership of a single variable?

Further reading

Packt has many other great resources for learning Rust:

- https://www.packtpub.com/application-development/rust-programming-example
- https://www.packtpub.com/application-development/learning-rust

For basic documentation and a tutorial, please refer here:

- Tutorial: https://doc.rust-lang.org/book/first-edition/
- Documentation: https://doc.rust-lang.org/stable/reference/

Functional Control Flow

2

The control flow is the most basic building block of programming. Early languages had no concept of data structures or functions, only program flow. These control flow structures have evolved over time, from simple branches and loops to the complex value expressions available in Rust.

In this chapter, we will start developing the project that will form the basis of all code examples in this book. The first project's requirements are introduced immediately. Then, we will provide you with actionable steps to transform project requirements into a code outline with tests. Lastly, we will develop code for the full deliverable.

Learning outcomes:

- Gathering project requirements
- Architecting a solution based on project requirements
- Using and recognizing expressions in functional style
- Testing the solution with integration and unit tests

Technical requirements

A recent version of Rust is necessary to run the examples provided:

```
https://www.rust-lang.org/en-US/install.html
```

This chapter's code is also available on GitHub:

```
https://github.com/PacktPublishing/Hands-On-Functional-Programming-in-RUST
```

Specific installation and build instructions are also included in each chapter's README.md file.

Designing the program

To design the program, let's look at the various aspects required for the project.

Gathering project requirements

Consider this situation: Your engineering firm is being considered for a contract to design software to control the elevators for a real estate developer. The contract lists three buildings under development with various heights and non-uniform elevator designs. The elevator designs are being finalized by other subcontractors and will become available shortly after the software contract is awarded.

To submit your proposal, your firm should demonstrate the basic capabilities of your elevator control software. Then, once awarded, you will be expected to integrate these capabilities into the final software, along with modifications that are necessary to accommodate the physical elevator specifications and behaviors.

To win the proposal, your team agrees on several key points on which to outperform competitors. Namely, your elevators should do the following:

- Take less time moving between floors
- Stop at each floor location more precisely
- Provide a smoother ride for passengers in transit

As a program deliverable to accompany the project proposal, you are expected to provide a simulation of elevator behavior. You are responsible for further details and implementation.

The following questions should be resolved now:

- What data will the program access and store?
- What input will the program expect?
- What output should the program produce?

After some deliberation, your team agrees on some behaviors:

- The program should emphasize the elevator's location, velocity, and acceleration. Velocity determines ride duration. Acceleration determines ride comfort. The location, at rest, determines stop precision. These are the key selling points that your company will emphasize, so the demonstration software should mirror the same message.

- As input, the program should take a file describing the number of floors and floor height, and finally a list of floor requests for the elevator to process.
- The output of the program should be real-time information regarding the elevator's location, velocity, and acceleration. After processing all floor requests, the program should print average and standard deviations for location, velocity, and acceleration.

Architecting a code map from requirements

To outline our code solution, we will use the `stubs` method. To use this process, we simply start a code project normally and fill out high-level details as we think of them. Details will be left unimplemented until we finalize the outline. After we are satisfied with the overall program design, then we can start implementing program logic. We will begin the project now.

Creating a Rust project

To create a new Rust project, we will perform the following steps (alternatively, you can invoke `cargo new`):

1. Create a new folder for the Rust project
2. Create a `Cargo.toml` file, which is shown as follows:

```
[package]
name = "elevator"
version = "1.0.0"

[dependencies]
```

3. Create a `src/main.rs` file, as follows:

```
fn main()
{
    println!("main")
}
```

Now, we can build the project with `cargo build`.

Writing stubs for each program requirement

Program requirements are typically phrased as outcomes. What effects should this program have when you run it? Answering this question with code is often straightforward. Here is a list of steps to methodically transform project requirements into code:

1. List all program requirements
2. List dependencies or prerequisites for each requirement
3. Create a dependency graph from the requirements and dependencies lists
4. Write stubs that implement the dependency graph

With practice, these steps can be combined into a single step of writing the stub code. However, if you become overwhelmed during the architecture phase of a project, then it may be helpful to go through these steps explicitly. This is a reliable method to break down complex problems into smaller problems:

1. Firstly, to list all program requirements, from earlier consideration, we know that we need to store real-time data for location, velocity, and acceleration. The program should accept an input file or standard input describing the number of floors, floor height, and a list of floor requests to be processed. The output of the program should be real-time elevator location, velocity, and acceleration, with a summary, upon completion, of all transport requests. The summary should list average and standard deviation for location, velocity, and acceleration.
2. Secondly, list dependencies or prerequisites for each requirement. The data seems to be atomic with no dependencies or prerequisites. The program flow seems to naturally take the form of a polling loop, updating real-time state information from sensors and issuing motion commands once per loop. There is a time-lagged circular dependency between elevator state and motion commands: motion commands are chosen based on state, and the next loop will realize the time-adjusted effect of those commands.
3. Thirdly, create a dependency graph from the requirements and dependencies lists with the following:
   1. Store the location, velocity, and acceleration state
   2. Store the motor input voltage
   3. Store the input building description and floor requests
   4. Parse the input and store as building description and floor requests

2. Loop while there are remaining floor requests:
   1. Update the location, velocity, and acceleration
   2. If the next floor request in the queue is satisfied, then remove it from the queue
   3. Adjust motor control to process the next floor request
   4. Print real-time statistics
3. Print the summary

2. Fourthly, write stubs that implement the dependency graph. We will update src/main.rs to implement this stub logic. Note that the variables, declared by let bindings, are stored inside the main function. The mutable state must be stored inside a function or a data structure. This is shown in the following code block:

```
pub fn run_simulation()
{

    //1. Store location, velocity, and acceleration state
    let mut location: f64 = 0.0; // meters
    let mut velocity: f64 = 0.0; // meters per second
    let mut acceleration: f64 = 0.0; // meters per second squared
    //2. Store motor input voltage
    let mut up_input_voltage: f64 = 0.0;
    let mut down_input_voltage: f64 = 0.0;

    //3. Store input building description and floor requests
    let mut floor_count: u64 = 0;
    let mut floor_height: f64 = 0.0; // meters
    let mut floor_requests: Vec<u64> = Vec::new();

    //4. Parse input and store as building description and floor
requests

    //5. Loop while there are remaining floor requests
    while floor_requests.len() > 0
    {
        //5.1. Update location, velocity, and acceleration

        //5.2. If next floor request in queue is satisfied, then
remove from queue

        //5.3. Adjust motor control to process next floor request

        //5.4. Print realtime statistics
    }
```

```
        //6. Print summary
        println!("summary");
    }

    fn main()
    {
        run_simulation()
    }
```

Alternatively, we could have written the loop as a separate function. The function would check the condition, and the function would potentially call itself again. When a function calls itself, this is called **recursion**. Recursion is an extremely common and important pattern in functional programming. However, this specific type of recursion, known as **tail recursion**, is not recommended in Rust currently (see RFC #271 (`https://github.com/rust-lang/rfcs/issues/271`)—without this proposed optimization, the tail recursion may unnecessarily use extra stack space and run out of memory).

The recursive loop code would become as follows:

```
    fn process_floor_requests(...)
    {
        if floor_requests.len() == 0 { return; }

        //5.1 Update location, velocity, and acceleration

        //5.2 If next floor request in queue is satisfied, then remove from
    queue

        //5.3 Adjust motor control to process next floor request

        //5.4 Print realtime statistics

        //tail recursion
        process_floor_requests(...)
    }
```

Implementing program logic

Once a stub program has been created, we can proceed to replace stubs with working code.

Filling in the blanks

Now that we have code stubs and a map of each feature that needs to be implemented, we can begin writing the code logic. At this point, if you are working on a team, then this would be a good time to divide the work. The architecture phase may be done by one person, or as a team, but it can't be done in parallel. In contrast, the implementation phase can be broken into parts to work on separately.

Parsing input and storing as building description and floor requests

To parse input, we first need to decide whether to expect input from stdin or from a file. We will adopt the convention that if a filename is provided to the program, then we will read from the file; if the file name is – then read from stdin, and otherwise read from test1.txt.

Using the Rust std::env package and a pattern match statement, we can accomplish this quite easily. This is shown as follows:

```
let buffer = match env::args().nth(1) {
    Some(ref fp) if *fp == "-".to_string()  => {
        let mut buffer = String::new();
        io::stdin().read_to_string(&mut buffer)
                .expect("read_to_string failed");
        buffer
    },
    None => {
        let fp = "test1.txt";
        let mut buffer = String::new();
        File::open(fp)
            .expect("File::open failed")
            .read_to_string(&mut buffer)
            .expect("read_to_string failed");
        buffer
    },
    Some(fp) => {
        let mut buffer = String::new();
        File::open(fp)
            .expect("File::open failed")
            .read_to_string(&mut buffer)
            .expect("read_to_string failed");
        buffer
    }
};
```

Now, we need to parse the string's input. For each line in the input, we store the parsed value as either a floor count, floor height, or floor request, in that order. Here is the code to implement this:

```
for (li,l) in buffer.lines().enumerate() {
    if li==0 {
        floor_count = l.parse::<u64>().unwrap();
    } else if li==1 {
        floor_height = l.parse::<f64>().unwrap();
    } else {
        floor_requests.push(l.parse::<u64>().unwrap());
    }
}
```

Updating location, velocity, and acceleration

Here, we need to update the program's state to reflect physical changes in the state variables since the previous loop iteration. All of these changes depend on knowledge of how much time has elapsed since the previous iteration, but we don't have that information store. So, let's make some small changes to our code.

1. Store a timestamp of the previous iteration outside of the loop:

   ```
   let mut prev_loop_time = Instant::now();
   ```

2. Calculate the elapsed time, then overwrite the previous timestamp:

   ```
   let now = Instant::now();
   let dt = now.duration_since(prev_loop_time)
               .as_fractional_secs();
   prev_loop_time = now;
   ```

3. To improve accuracy, sleep for a while at the end of the loop (it is difficult to accurately record sub-millisecond measurements):

   ```
   thread::sleep(time::Duration::from_millis(10));
   ```

Now, we can start to calculate the new location, velocity, and acceleration. The location is calculated as previous location plus velocity over time. Velocity is calculated as previous velocity plus acceleration over time. Acceleration is calculated as *F=ma* and will be calculated from the motor force and carriage weight. At this point, we realize that carriage weight is not specified in the input file, but after some discussion, the team decides to use a standard carriage weight rather than change the input format.

With a little research, you find that an elevator carriage weighs about 1,200 kg. Similarly, you estimate that a simple DC motor can produce roughly eight newtons of force per volt. The resulting code looks like the following:

```
location = location + velocity * dt;
velocity = velocity + acceleration * dt;
acceleration = {
    let F = (up_input_voltage - down_input_voltage) * 8.0;
    let m = 1200000.0;
    //-9.8 is an approximation of acceleration due to gravity
    -9.8 + F/m
};
```

If the next floor request in the queue is satisfied, then remove it from the queue

To complete a floor request, we must be at the destination floor and stopped. We assume that a sufficiently low velocity can be stopped with some sort of brake. This will hold us in place steadily until passengers depart or enter the elevator. The code is as follows:

```
let next_floor = floor_requests[0];
if (location - (next_floor as f64)*floor_height).abs() < 0.01
    && velocity.abs() < 0.01
{
    velocity = 0.0;
    floor_requests.remove(0);
}
```

Adjusting motor control to process the next floor request

To adjust motor control, we need to decide how much acceleration we want, and then calculate how much force is required to achieve the target acceleration. According to our objectives, we want shorter travel time, less motion sickness, and accurate stop locations.

The metrics that we should optimize to achieve these objectives are to maximize average velocity, minimize acceleration, and minimize stop location error. All of these objectives compete with one another for precedence, so we will need to compromise between each to achieve good overall performance.

With some research, you find that comfortable acceleration is limited to between 1 and 1.5 meters per second squared. You decide to aim for a maximum of 1 m/s^2, with a slack of up to 1.5 m/s^2 in exceptional circumstances.

For velocity, you decide that carriage speeds over 5 m/s are unsafe, so you will implement a maximum velocity, otherwise, the velocity should always be maximized to reach the next floor.

For location precision, the calculation of target acceleration versus current velocity versus target destination is essential. Here, you will try to keep the acceleration near 1 m/s^2, with significant room for additional acceleration. When sufficiently close to the destination, it may be necessary to use a different acceleration target to make smaller motions and velocity adjustments.

To implement this with code, we first calculate the deceleration range. This is defined as the distance from which, at the current velocity, we would need to decelerate at greater than 1 m/s^2 to stop at the destination. Our acceleration buffer provides some room for correction, making this a safe target from which to start decelerating before reaching the next floor. This is shown in the following code:

```
//it will take t seconds to decelerate from velocity v at -1 m/s^2
let t = velocity.abs() / 1.0;

//during which time, the carriage will travel d=t * v/2 meters
//at an average velocity of v/2 before stopping
let d = t * (velocity/2.0);

//l = distance to next floor
let l = (location - (next_floor as f64)*floor_height).abs();
```

To calculate the target acceleration, we have three cases to consider:

- If we are in the deceleration range, then we should slow down
- If we are not in the deceleration range and not at maximum velocity, then we should accelerate
- If we are outside of the deceleration range but already at maximum velocity, then we should not change velocity:

```
let target_acceleration = {
    //are we going up?
    let going_up = location < (next_floor as f64)*floor_height;

    //Do not exceed maximum velocity
    if velocity.abs() >= 5.0 {
        //if we are going up and actually going up
        //or we are going down and actually going down
        if (going_up && velocity>0.0)
        || (!going_up && velocity<0.0) {
            0.0
        //decelerate if going in wrong direction
        } else if going_up {
            1.0
        } else {
            -1.0
        }

    //if within comfortable deceleration range and moving in right
direction, decelerate
    } else if l < d && going_up==(velocity>0.0) {
        if going_up {
            -1.0
        } else {
            1.0
        }

    //else if not at peak velocity, accelerate
    } else {
        if going_up {
            1.0
        } else {
            -1.0
        }
    }
};
```

Finally, using the target acceleration, we can calculate how much voltage we should apply to each motor to achieve the desired acceleration. By inverting the formula previously used to calculate acceleration, we can now calculate our desired voltage from the target acceleration, as follows:

```
let gravity_adjusted_acceleration = target_acceleration + 9.8;
let target_force = gravity_adjusted_acceleration * 1200000.0;
let target_voltage = target_force / 8.0;
if target_voltage > 0.0 {
    up_input_voltage = target_voltage;
    down_input_voltage = 0.0;
} else {
    up_input_voltage = 0.0;
    down_input_voltage = target_voltage.abs();
};
```

Printing real-time statistics

To print real-time statistics, we will use a console formatting library. This allows us to easily move the cursor around the screen and write clear and easily formattable text. This is depicted as follows:

1. To get started, we should grab some information and a handle to `stdout` and store it outside of our loop. This is shown in the following code:

```
let termsize = termion::terminal_size().ok();
let termwidth = termsize.map(|(w,_)| w-2).expect("termwidth");
let termheight = termsize.map(|(_,h)|
h-2).expect("termheight");
let mut _stdout = io::stdout(); //lock once, instead of once
per write
let mut stdout = _stdout.lock().into_raw_mode().unwrap();
```

2. Inside the loop, let's start by clearing a space to render our output:

```
print!("{}{}", clear::All, cursor::Goto(1, 1));
for tx in 0..(termwidth-1)
{
    for ty in 0..(termheight-1)
    {
        write!(stdout, "{}", cursor::Goto(tx+1, ty+1));
        write!(stdout, "{}", " ");
    }
}
```

3. Then, we can render the elevator shaft and carriage. The elevator shaft will be simple brackets, one for each floor on the left and right. The elevator carriage will be an X mark placed on the floor closest to the current carriage location. We calculate each floor location by multiplying `floor_height` by floor offset from the ground floor. Then, we compare each floor location to the carriage locations to find the closest one. The code is as follows:

```
print!("{}{}{}", clear::All, cursor::Goto(1, 1), cursor::Hide);
let carriage_floor = (location / floor_height).floor() as u64;
let carriage_floor = cmp::max(carriage_floor, 0);
let carriage_floor = cmp::min(carriage_floor, floor_count-1);
for tx in 0..(termwidth-1)
{
    for ty in 0..(termheight-1)
    {
        write!(stdout, "{}", cursor::Goto(tx+1, ty+1));
        if tx==0 && (ty as u64)<floor_count {
            write!(stdout, "{}", "[");
        } else if tx==1 && (ty as u64)==((floor_count-1)-
carriage_floor) {
            write!(stdout, "{}", "X");
        } else if tx==2 && (ty as u64)<floor_count {
            write!(stdout, "{}", "]");
        } else {
            write!(stdout, "{}", " ");
        }
    }
}
stdout.flush().unwrap();
```

4. Now, we need to print real-time statistics. In addition to location, velocity, and acceleration, let's also display the nearest floor and motor input voltage, as follows:

```
write!(stdout, "{}", cursor::Goto(6, 1));
write!(stdout, "Carriage at floor {}", carriage_floor+1);
write!(stdout, "{}", cursor::Goto(6, 2));
write!(stdout, "Location          {}", location);
write!(stdout, "{}", cursor::Goto(6, 3));
write!(stdout, "Velocity          {}", velocity);
write!(stdout, "{}", cursor::Goto(6, 4));
write!(stdout, "Acceleration      {}", acceleration);
write!(stdout, "{}", cursor::Goto(6, 5));
write!(stdout, "Voltage [up-down] {}", up_input_voltage-
down_input_voltage);
```

5. Here, we find that the Terminal screen is tearing, so let's adjust the output to use a buffer:

```
let mut terminal_buffer = vec![' ' as u8; (termwidth*termheight) as
usize];
for ty in 0..floor_count
{
    terminal_buffer[ (ty*termwidth + 0) as usize ] = '[' as u8;
    terminal_buffer[ (ty*termwidth + 1) as usize ] =
        if    (ty as u64)==((floor_count-1)-carriage_floor) { 'X' as u8 }
        else { ' ' as u8 };
    terminal_buffer[ (ty*termwidth + 2) as usize ] = ']' as u8;
    terminal_buffer[ (ty*termwidth + termwidth-2) as usize ] = '\r' as
u8;
    terminal_buffer[ (ty*termwidth + termwidth-1) as usize ] = '\n' as
u8;
}
let stats = vec![
    format!("Carriage at floor {}", carriage_floor+1),
    format!("Location        {}", location),
    format!("Velocity        {}", velocity),
    format!("Acceleration    {}", acceleration),
    format!("Voltage [up-down] {}", up_input_voltage-down_input_voltage)
];
for sy in 0..stats.len()
{
    for (sx,sc) in stats[sy].chars().enumerate()
    {
        terminal_buffer[ sy*(termwidth as usize) + 6 + sx ] = sc as u8;
    }
}
write!(stdout, "{}", String::from_utf8(terminal_buffer).unwrap());
```

Now, our screen will clearly display real-time information until the loop ends.

Printing summary

To print our summary, we should include averages and standard deviations for location, velocity, and acceleration. Additionally, it may be interesting to see statistics for motor control, so let's also display voltage statistics. At this point, we realize that the data is not storing enough information to calculate average or standard deviation numbers.

To calculate the average value for a variable, we will need to calculate a sum of each recorded value and record a count of how many data points we recorded. Then, we will calculate the average value by dividing the total value by the record count, giving us our estimation of the average value over time.

To calculate the standard deviation, we will require a full record of each observed value of the variable. Additionally, the average value and record count are required. Then, we will use the following formula to calculate standard deviation:

$$\sqrt{\frac{\sum_{i=1}^{N}(x_i - \bar{x})^2}{N - 1}}$$

To store our data, we need to declare new variables before our loop starts:

1. To store data using new variables, use the following code:

```
let mut record_location = Vec::new();
let mut record_velocity = Vec::new();
let mut record_acceleration = Vec::new();
let mut record_voltage = Vec::new();
```

2. Then, at each iteration, before calculating the new values, we will store each data point:

```
record_location.push(location);
record_velocity.push(velocity);
record_acceleration.push(acceleration);
record_voltage.push(up_input_voltage-down_input_voltage);
```

3. Finally, we calculate the statistics:

```
let record_location_N = record_location.len();
let record_location_sum: f64 = record_location.iter().sum();
let record_location_avg = record_location_sum / (record_location_N
as f64);
let record_location_dev = (
    record_location.clone().into_iter()
    .map(|v| (v - record_location_avg).powi(2))
    .fold(0.0, |a, b| a+b)
    / (record_location_N as f64)
).sqrt();

let record_velocity_N = record_velocity.len();
let record_velocity_sum: f64 = record_velocity.iter().sum();
let record_velocity_avg = record_velocity_sum / (record_velocity_N
```

```
as f64);
let record_velocity_dev = (
    record_velocity.clone().into_iter()
    .map(|v| (v - record_velocity_avg).powi(2))
    .fold(0.0, |a, b| a+b)
    / (record_velocity_N as f64)
).sqrt();

let record_acceleration_N = record_acceleration.len();
let record_acceleration_sum: f64 =
record_acceleration.iter().sum();
let record_acceleration_avg = record_acceleration_sum /
(record_acceleration_N as f64);
let record_acceleration_dev = (
    record_acceleration.clone().into_iter()
    .map(|v| (v - record_acceleration_avg).powi(2))
    .fold(0.0, |a, b| a+b)
    / (record_acceleration_N as f64)
).sqrt();

let record_voltage_N = record_voltage.len();
let record_voltage_sum = record_voltage.iter().sum();
let record_voltage_avg = record_voltage_sum / (record_voltage_N as
f64);
let record_voltage_dev = (
    record_voltage.clone().into_iter()
    .map(|v| (v - record_voltage_avg).powi(2))
    .fold(0.0, |a, b| a+b)
    / (record_voltage_N as f64)
).sqrt();
```

4. Before exiting the program, we must print the statistics:

```
write!(stdout, "{}{}{}", clear::All, cursor::Goto(1, 1),
cursor::Show).unwrap();

write!(stdout, "Average of location              {:.6}\r\n",
record_location_avg);
write!(stdout, "Standard deviation of location   {:.6}\r\n",
record_location_dev);
write!(stdout, "\r\n");

write!(stdout, "Average of velocity              {:.6}\r\n",
record_velocity_avg);
write!(stdout, "Standard deviation of velocity   {:.6}\r\n",
record_velocity_dev);
write!(stdout, "\r\n");
```

```
write!(stdout, "Average of acceleration           {:.6}\r\n",
record_acceleration_avg);
write!(stdout, "Standard deviation of acceleration {:.6}\r\n",
record_acceleration_dev);
write!(stdout, "\r\n");

write!(stdout, "Average of voltage                {:.6}\r\n",
record_voltage_avg);
write!(stdout, "Standard deviation of voltage      {:.6}\r\n",
record_voltage_dev);
write!(stdout, "\r\n");

stdout.flush().unwrap();
```

Now, having assembled the pieces, we have a complete simulation. Running the program on a test input produces a nice graphic and result summary. This should be sufficient to accompany the initial proposal.

Breaking down long segments into components

Once the project is functional, we can begin to look for opportunities to simplify the design and eliminate redundancies. The first step here should be to look for patterns of similar code. Our summary statistics are a very good example of code that should be cleaned up. We have four variables that we track and display statistics for. The calculation of each statistic is identical, yet we repeat the calculation explicitly for each variable. There are also similarities in the output formatting, so let's also clean that up.

To fix redundancy, the first question to ask is whether the code can be rewritten as a function. Here, we do have the opportunity to use this pattern by creating a function that accepts the variable data and prints the summary. This is done as follows:

1. We can write this function, which is shown as follows:

```
fn variable_summary<W: Write>(stdout: &mut raw::RawTerminal<W>,
vname: &str, data: Vec<f64>)
{
    //calculate statistics
    let N = data.len();
    let sum: f64 = data.iter().sum();
    let avg = sum / (N as f64);
    let dev = (
        data.clone().into_iter()
        .map(|v| (v - avg).powi(2))
        .fold(0.0, |a, b| a+b)
```

```
        / (N as f64)
    ).sqrt();

    //print formatted output
    write!(stdout, "Average of {:25}{:.6}\r\n", vname, avg);
    write!(stdout, "Standard deviation of {:14}{:.6}\r\n", vname,
dev);
    write!(stdout, "\r\n");
}
```

2. To call the function, we provide each `name` and `data` variable:

```
write!(stdout, "{}{}{}", clear::All, cursor::Goto(1, 1),
cursor::Show).unwrap();
variable_summary(&mut stdout, "location", record_location);
variable_summary(&mut stdout, "velocity", record_velocity);
variable_summary(&mut stdout, "acceleration", record_acceleration);
variable_summary(&mut stdout, "voltage", record_voltage);
stdout.flush().unwrap();
```

This rewrite improves the program in two significant ways:

- The statistics calculation is much easier to read and debug
- Using the statistics and summary function involves very little redundancy, which reduces the likelihood of accidentally using incorrect variable names or other common errors

Short, literate code is robust and prevents mistakes. Long, redundant code is brittle and error-prone.

Searching for abstractions

After writing a code draft, it is a good practice to read through the code again and look for possible improvements. When reviewing a project, look specifically for ugly code, anti-patterns, and unchecked assumptions. After review, we find the code does not need correcting.

We should, however, point out one functional abstraction that was used that reduced line count significantly, which is the use of iterators. In calculating our variable summaries, we always used iterators to calculate sums and statistics. Some of the operators have not been introduced, so let's look closer:

```
let N = data.len();
let sum: f64 = data.iter().sum();
let avg = sum / (N as f64);
let dev = (
    data.clone().into_iter()
    .map(|v| (v - avg).powi(2))
    .fold(0.0, |a, b| a+b)
    / (N as f64)
).sqrt();
```

Here, there are two important iterator methods being used—map and fold. map accept a mapping function and return an iterator of the modified values. The fold method holds an accumulator value (argument 1), and, for each element in the iterator, applies the accumulator function (argument 2), returning the accumulated value as a result. The fold function consumes the iterator when called.

An iterator is defined by a trait with a next method, which may return the next item in the sequence. A simple infinite list could be defined as follows:

```
struct Fibonacci
{
 curr: u32,
 next: u32,
}

impl Iterator for Fibonacci
{
    type Item = u32;
    fn next(&mut self) -> Option<u32>
    {
        let new_next = self.curr + self.next;
        self.curr = self.next;
        self.next = new_next;
        Some(self.curr) //infinite list, never None
    }
}

fn fibonacci() -> Fibonacci
{
    Fibonacci { curr: 1, next: 1 }
}
```

These objects define an iterator. The `map` function and other stream modifiers simply wrap the input stream inside of another iterator that applies the modifier.

Alternatively, the statistics calculation could have been defined with `for` loops. The result would look like the following:

```
let N = data.len();
let mut sum = 0.0;
for di in 0..data.len()
{
    sum += data[di];
}
let avg = sum / (N as f64);
let mut dev = 0.0;
for di in 0..data.len()
{
    dev += (data[di] - avg).powi(2);
}
dev = (dev / (N as f64)).sqrt();
```

By comparison, we can see that the functional code is a little bit shorter. More importantly, the functional code is declarative. When code only describes requirements, we call that code **declarative**. When code describes machine instructions to satisfy requirements, we call that code **imperative**. The primary benefits of declarative style over imperative style are that declarative style is self-documenting and prevents mistakes by making them more obvious.

For these reasons, when searching for abstractions, we encourage looking at `for` loops. In most cases, `for` loops can be messy or otherwise undesirable. Iterators and combinators may be a good solution to help improve code quality.

Writing tests

To run tests from the command line, type `cargo test`. We will be doing this a lot.

Unit testing

Unit testing focuses on testing internal interfaces and components of a program. It is also called **whitebox testing**. To first create unit tests, it is a good idea to look at all of the top-level types, traits, and functions. All top-level identifiers make for good test cases. Depending on the structure of the program, it may also be a good idea to test combinations of these components to cover expected use cases.

We have one utility function, the statistic calculation, which would be a good candidate to write a unit test for. However, this function doesn't return any result. Instead, it immediately prints output to the console. To test this, we should break the function into two components—one that calculates the statistics, and a second function that prints the statistics. This would look as follows:

```
fn variable_summary<W: Write>(stdout: &mut raw::RawTerminal<W>, vname:
&str, data: Vec<f64>)
{
    let (avg, dev) = variable_summary_stats(data);
    variable_summary_print(stdout, vname, avg, dev);
}

fn variable_summary_stats(data: Vec<f64>) -> (f64, f64)
{
    //calculate statistics
    let N = data.len();
    let sum: f64 = data.iter().sum();
    let avg = sum / (N as f64);
    let dev = (
        data.clone().into_iter()
        .map(|v| (v - avg).powi(2))
        .fold(0.0, |a, b| a+b)
        / (N as f64)
    ).sqrt();
    (avg, dev)
}

fn variable_summary_print<W: Write>(stdout: &mut raw::RawTerminal<W>,
vname: &str, avg: f64, dev: f64)
{
    //print formatted output
```

```
        write!(stdout, "Average of {:25}{:.6}\r\n", vname, avg);
        write!(stdout, "Standard deviation of {:14}{:.6}\r\n", vname, dev);
        write!(stdout, "\r\n");
}
```

Now that we have isolated the statistics calculation into its own function, we can write unit tests for it much more easily. First, we supply some test data, and then verify each result. Also note that unit tests have access to private functions as long as we add use super::*; to the test declaration. Here are some unit tests for our statistics calculation:

```
#[cfg(test)]
mod tests {
    use super::*;

    #[test]
    fn variable_stats() {
        let test_data = vec![
            (vec![1.0, 2.0, 3.0, 4.0, 5.0], 3.0, 1.41),
            (vec![1.0, 3.0, 5.0, 7.0, 9.0], 5.0, 2.83),
            (vec![1.0, 9.0, 1.0, 9.0, 1.0], 4.2, 3.92),
            (vec![1.0, 0.5, 0.7, 0.9, 0.6], 0.74, 0.19),
            (vec![200.0, 3.0, 24.0, 92.0, 111.0], 86.0, 69.84),
        ];
        for (data, avg, dev) in test_data
        {
            let (ravg, rdev) = variable_summary_stats(data);
            //it is not safe to use direct == operator on floats
            //floats can be *very* close and not equal
            //so instead we check that they are very close in value
            assert!( (avg-ravg).abs() < 0.1 );
            assert!( (dev-rdev).abs() < 0.1 );
        }
    }
}
```

Now, if we run cargo test, the unit tests will run. The result should show one test passing.

Integration testing

Integration testing focuses on testing external interfaces of a program. It is also called **blackbox testing**. To create integration tests, focus on what the input and output of a program or module should be. Think of the different configurations of options, data, and possible internal interactions to create tests. These tests should then provide good coverage of high-level behavior of the completed program.

To create an integration test, we first need to reconfigure our project as a module that can be imported. Integration tests do not have access to symbols other than what they can reference from use statements. To accomplish this, we can move the program logic into a `src/lib.rs` file and use a simple wrapper for `src/main.rs`. After this change, the `lib.rs` file should contain all of the code from `main.rs`, with the one change of renaming the `main` function to `run_simulation` and making the function public. The `main.rs` wrapper should then look as follows:

```
extern crate elevator;

fn main()
{
    elevator::run_simulation();
}
```

Now, in order to create an integration test:

1. Create a `tests/` directory
2. Create an `integration_tests.rs` file inside the `tests/` directory
3. Inside the `integration_tests.rs` file, create functions for each test case

We will create a single test case here to accept a specific elevator request and check that the requests are processed in a reasonable amount of time. The test harness is as follows:

```
extern crate elevator;
extern crate timebomb;
use timebomb::timeout_ms;

#[test]
fn test_main() {
    timeout_ms(|| {
        elevator::run_simulation();
    }, 300000);
}
```

As input, we will use a 5 story building, 5.67 meters for each floor, and 7 floor requests. The file will be stored as test1.txt and should have the following structure:

```
5
5.67
2
1
4
0
3
1
0
```

With these tests in place, we can now confirm that the basic logic is working and that the program as a whole function properly. To run all tests, call cargo test, or use a specific test case with cargo test casename.

A sample test run is as follows:

```
[ ]     Carriage at floor 1
[ ]     Location          2.203829
[ ]     Velocity          -2.157214
[ ]     Acceleration      1.000000
[X]     Voltage [up-down] 1620000.000000

[ ]     Carriage at floor 3
[ ]     Location          11.344785
[X]     Velocity          0.173572
[ ]     Acceleration      -1.000000
[ ]     Voltage [up-down] 1320000.000000

[ ]     Carriage at floor 4
[X]     Location          19.235710
[ ]     Velocity          2.669347
[ ]     Acceleration      -1.000000
[ ]     Voltage [up-down] 1320000.000000

[ ]     Carriage at floor 1
[ ]     Location          0.133051
[ ]     Velocity          0.160799
[ ]     Acceleration      -1.000000
[X]     Voltage [up-down] 1320000.000000
```

Once the simulation completes, the summary and test results are as follows:

```
Average of location                5.017036
Standard deviation of location      8.813507

Average of velocity                -0.007597
Standard deviation of velocity      2.107692

Average of acceleration             0.000850
Standard deviation of acceleration  0.995623

Average of voltage                  1470109.838195
Standard deviation of voltage       149352.287579

test test_main ... ok

test result: ok. 1 passed; 0 failed; 0 ignored; 0 measured; 0 filtered out

running 1 test
test tests::variable_stats ... ok

test result: ok. 1 passed; 0 failed; 0 ignored; 0 measured; 0 filtered out
```

Summary

In this chapter, we outlined the steps taken to gather project requirements, architect a solution, and then implement the completed deliverable. We focused on how this process can be clarified using functional thinking.

When gathering program requirements, the required data, input, and output should be clarified. When translating requirements into a code plan, creating a dependency graph as an intermediary step can help simplify complex designs. When testing, functions become great units to cover. By comparison, lines and lines of imperative code are almost impossible to test.

We will continue to develop this software project throughout the book. This first simulation deliverable will accompany the project proposal and will hopefully help our firm be selected for the contract. In the next chapter, you will receive feedback from the developers and meet your competitor.

Questions

1. What is the ternary operator?
2. What is another name for unit tests?
3. What is another name for integration tests?
4. What is declarative programming?
5. What is imperative programming?
6. What is defined in the iterator trait?
7. In which direction will fold traverse the iterator sequence?
8. What is a dependency graph?
9. What are the two constructors of `Option`?

3
Functional Data Structures

Data structures are the second most basic building blocks of programming, following control flow. After early languages developed control flow structures, it quickly became apparent that simple variable labels were insufficient for developing complex programs. Data structures have evolved from the basic concept of a sized datum stored at an address to the concept of strings and arrays, followed by mixed structures, and finally collections.

In this chapter, we will revisit the project introduced in `Chapter 2`, *Functional Control Flow*. The project requirements have expanded to accommodate feedback from the potential client. There are also specific performance targets that must be met due to competition from a rival developer. To help our business succeed, we must now improve the previous simulation and ensure that it meets customer demand and performance targets.

In this chapter, we will cover the following:

- Adjusting to changing the scope of the project
- Reformatting code to support multiple use cases
- Using appropriate data structures to gather, store, and process data
- Organizing code into traits and data classes

Technical requirements

A recent version of Rust is necessary to run the examples provided:

```
https://www.rust-lang.org/en-US/install.html
```

This chapter's code is also available on GitHub:

```
https://github.com/PacktPublishing/Hands-On-Functional-Programming-in-RUST
```

Specific installation and build instructions are also included in each chapter's `README.md` file.

Adjusting to changing the scope of the project

You can't plan for everything. You also probably don't want to try to plan for everything. Flexible software development and emphasizing robust, logically independent components will reduce work when a requirement or dependency inevitably changes.

Gathering new project requirements

After an initial demonstration, your team has received comments and feedback from the potential client. Watching the simulation, the elevator seems to often pass and go back up to floors before stopping. The client expressed concern that this would be not only inefficient, but also uncomfortable or irritable for passengers. To win the contract, the client wants to see improvements and evidence showing that:

- The ride is comfortable and reliably direct
- The ride moves efficiently from each source to each destination floor

Additionally, you have learned that a competitor has submitted a separate proposal. The competitor specifically claims that its elevator control system maintains acceleration within comfortable levels, velocity within safe bounds, and reaches destinations accurately within 20% of physical theoretical limits. No specific numbers were provided, and no simulation was demonstrated, but the client seemed very convinced, along with the assurance that the project will cost 10% less.

Architecting a change map from requirements

After receiving feedback and new expectations, we must convert these demands into a plan of action. The simulation needs to be updated and additional tools will need to be built. Let's review the new information and architect a solution to meet the new requirements.

Translating expectations into requirements

Reviewing the feedback, it is clear that there are two perspectives that need to be addressed:

- A competitor has made specific claims that our company will need to outperform
- The client has explicit expectations to address concerns from the first demonstration

The specific claims from the competitor can be listed as follows:

- Acceleration is within comfortable bounds
- Velocity is within safe bounds
- Trip time from any floor to any other floor is within 20% of physical theoretical limits
- The software is 10% cheaper

We will delegate the price negotiation to our sales team, but otherwise we need to adjust our software to outperform the other three claims. If we can meet these requirements and provide adequate supporting evidence, then this should also address most of the client's explicit concerns.

Additionally, the client was specifically concerned about the elevator passing the destination floor and needing to back up. We should address this behavior and confirm that it does not occur in simulations.

It is clear at this point that the previous motor control logic is inadequate. After brainstorming, your team develops two possible improvements:

- Use a variable acceleration/deceleration calculation, rather than on/off adjustment
- Reduce the update interval to permit faster and, thus, more precise decisions

Translating requirements into a change map

Given the various new requirements, it seems appropriate to split the previous simulation code into different libraries and executables. We will create a separate module for each of the following:

- A physics simulator
- A motor control
- An executable to run the simulation for demonstration
- An executable to further analyze the simulation

The physics simulator should accept a generic motor controller and a measurement accumulator. The measurement accumulator provided will accept readings of velocity, acceleration, and all other information available to the simulator. The motor controller provided will accept similar readings of velocity and so on, and produce an output of the desired voltage to motors. The resulting function will be responsible for accurately simulating the physical operation of any specified elevator and building.

The motor control will couple with the simulator, or eventually the actual elevator, to use available information to decide how to operate the elevator.

The simulation executable will wrap the physics simulator and motor control to create a program equivalent to the simulation from Chapter 2, *Functional Control Flow*. Additionally, all recorded information from the simulation should be saved to a file for further detailed analysis.

The analysis executable should accept the simulator trace file and check that all performance requirements have been met. Additionally, any analysis that would be useful for development purposes will be added here.

Mapping requirements directly to code

It is not always desirable to go through the full process of creating a dependency graph and pseudo code for each project or change. Here, we will transition directly from the preceding plan to the following code stubs.

Writing the physics simulator

The physics simulator in `src/physics.rs` is responsible for modeling the physics and layout of the building and elevator operations. The simulator will be provided with one object to handle motor control and another to handle data collection. The physics simulator module will define traits for each of those interfaces, and the motor control and data collection objects should implement each `trait`, respectively.

Let's start by defining some of the type declarations for the `physics` module. First, let's look at a key interface—the direct motor input. Until this point, we have assumed that motor input will have simple voltage control that we can represent as a positive or negative floating point integer. This definition is problematic, mainly in the sense that all references to this type will reference `f64`. This type specifies a very specific data representation with no room for adjustment. If we litter our code with references to this type, then any changes will require us to go back and edit every one of the references.

Instead, for the motor input type, let's provide a name for the type. This could be an alias for the `f64` type, which would solve the immediate concern. Though this is acceptable, we will choose to be even more explicit with the type definition and provide `enum` cases for up and down. The `enum` type, also known as a **tagged union**, is useful to define data that may have multiple structures or use cases. Here, the constructors are identical, but the meaning of each voltage field is opposite.

Furthermore, when interacting with the `MotorInput` type, we should avoid assuming any internal structure. This minimizes our exposure to future interface changes that may change because `MotorInput` defines an interface with a currently unknown physical component. We will be responsible for software compatibility with that interface. So, to abstract any interaction with `MotorInput`, we will use traits instead. Traits that do not define intrinsic behavior of a type, but rather associated behavior, are sometimes called **data classes**.

Here is the `enum` and a data class defining the calculation of force derived from an input:

```
#[derive(Clone,Serialize,Deserialize,Debug)]
pub enum MotorInput
{
    Up { voltage: f64 },
    Down { voltage: f64 }
}

pub trait MotorForce {
    fn calculate_force(&self) -> f64;
}
```

```
impl MotorForce for MotorInput {
   fn calculate_force(&self) -> f64
   {
      match *self {
         MotorInput::Up { voltage: v } => { v * 8.0 }
         MotorInput::Down { voltage: v } => { v * -8.0 }
      }
   }
}

pub trait MotorVoltage {
   fn voltage(&self) -> f64;
}

impl MotorVoltage for MotorInput {
   fn voltage(&self) -> f64
   {
      match *self {
         MotorInput::Up { voltage: v } => { v }
         MotorInput::Down { voltage: v } => { -v }
      }
   }
}
```

Next, let's define the elevator information. We will create an `ElevatorSpecification`, which describes the structure of the building and elevator. We also require an `ElevatorState` to hold information regarding the current elevator status. To clarify usage of floor requests, we will also create an alias for `FloorRequests` vectors to make the meaning explicit. We will choose to use a `struct` instead of tuples here to create explicit field names. Otherwise, structs and tuples are interchangeable for storing miscellaneous data. The definitions are as follows:

```
#[derive(Clone,Serialize,Deserialize,Debug)]
pub struct ElevatorSpecification
{
   pub floor_count: u64,
   pub floor_height: f64,
   pub carriage_weight: f64
}

#[derive(Clone,Serialize,Deserialize,Debug)]
pub struct ElevatorState
{
   pub timestamp: f64,
   pub location: f64,
   pub velocity: f64,
```

```
    pub acceleration: f64,
    pub motor_input: MotorInput
}

pub type FloorRequests = Vec<u64>;
```

The traits for MotorController and DataRecorder are almost identical. The only
difference is that polling a MotorController expects a MotorInput to be returned. Here,
we choose to use init methods instead of constructors to permit additional external
initialization of each resource. For example, it may be necessary for DataRecorder to open
files or other resources to be accessed during simulation. Here are the trait definitions:

```
pub trait MotorController
{
    fn init(&mut self, esp: ElevatorSpecification, est: ElevatorState);
    fn poll(&mut self, est: ElevatorState, dst: u64) -> MotorInput;
}

pub trait DataRecorder
{
    fn init(&mut self, esp: ElevatorSpecification, est: ElevatorState);
    fn poll(&mut self, est: ElevatorState, dst: u64);
    fn summary(&mut self);
}
```

To simulate the physics of the elevator, we will reproduce the central loop of the simulation
from Chapter 2, *Functional Control Flow*. Some of the state has been organized into
structures instead of loose variables. Motor control decisions have been delegated to the
MotorController object. Output and data recording has been delegated to the
DataRecorder. There is also a new parameter field to specify the elevator's carriage
weight. With all of these generalizations, the code becomes as follows:

```
pub fn simulate_elevator<MC: MotorController, DR: DataRecorder>(esp:
ElevatorSpecification, est: ElevatorState, req: FloorRequests,
                    mc: &mut MC, dr: &mut DR) {

    //immutable input becomes mutable local state
    let mut esp = esp.clone();
    let mut est = est.clone();
    let mut req = req.clone();

    //initialize MotorController and DataController
    mc.init(esp.clone(), est.clone());
    dr.init(esp.clone(), est.clone());

    //5. Loop while there are remaining floor requests
```

```
let original_ts = Instant::now();
thread::sleep(time::Duration::from_millis(1));
while req.len() > 0
{
   //5.1. Update location, velocity, and acceleration
   let now = Instant::now();
   let ts = now.duration_since(original_ts)
              .as_fractional_secs();
   let dt = ts - est.timestamp;
   est.timestamp = ts;

   est.location = est.location + est.velocity * dt;
   est.velocity = est.velocity + est.acceleration * dt;
   est.acceleration = {
      let F = est.motor_input.calculate_force();
      let m = esp.carriage_weight;
      -9.8 + F/m
   };
```

After declaring the state and calculating time-dependent variables, we add the elevator control logic:

```
   //5.2. If next floor request in queue is satisfied,
      then remove from queue
   let next_floor = req[0];
   if (est.location - (next_floor as f64)*esp.floor_height).abs()
      < 0.01 &&
      est.velocity.abs() < 0.01
   {
      est.velocity = 0.0;
      req.remove(0);
    //remove is an O(n) operation
    //Vec should not be used like this for large data
   }

   //5.4. Print realtime statistics
   dr.poll(est.clone(), next_floor);

   //5.3. Adjust motor control to process next floor request
   est.motor_input = mc.poll(est.clone(), next_floor);

   thread::sleep(time::Duration::from_millis(1));
   }
}
```

Writing the motor controller

The motor controllers in `src/motor.rs` will be responsible for making decisions regarding how much force to generate from the motor. The physics driver will supply current state information regarding all known measurements of location, velocity, and so on. Currently, the motor controller uses only the most current information to make control decisions. However, this may change in the future, in which case the controller may store past measurements.

Extracting the same control algorithm from the previous chapter, the new `MotorController` definition becomes as follows:

```rust
pub struct SimpleMotorController
{
    pub esp: ElevatorSpecification
}

impl MotorController for SimpleMotorController
{
    fn init(&mut self, esp: ElevatorSpecification, est: ElevatorState)
    {
        self.esp = esp;
    }

    fn poll(&mut self, est: ElevatorState, dst: u64) -> MotorInput
    {
        //5.3. Adjust motor control to process next floor request

        //it will take t seconds to decelerate from velocity v
          at -1 m/s^2
        let t = est.velocity.abs() / 1.0;

        //during which time, the carriage will travel d=t * v/2 meters
        //at an average velocity of v/2 before stopping
        let d = t * (est.velocity/2.0);

        //l = distance to next floor
        let l = (est.location - (dst as
            f64)*self.esp.floor_height).abs();
```

After establishing basic constants and values, we need to determine the target acceleration:

```
let target_acceleration = {
    //are we going up?
    let going_up = est.location < (dst as
        f64)*self.esp.floor_height;

    //Do not exceed maximum velocity
    if est.velocity.abs() >= 5.0 {
        if going_up==(est.velocity>0.0) {
            0.0
        //decelerate if going in wrong direction
        } else if going_up {
            1.0
        } else {
            -1.0
        }

    //if within comfortable deceleration range and moving
        in right direction, decelerate
    } else if l < d && going_up==(est.velocity>0.0) {
        if going_up {
            -1.0
        } else {
            1.0
        }

    //else if not at peak velocity, accelerate
    } else {
        if going_up {
            1.0
        } else {
            -1.0
        }
    }
};
```

After determining the target acceleration, it should be converted into a `MotorInput` value:

```
let gravity_adjusted_acceleration = target_acceleration + 9.8;
let target_force = gravity_adjusted_acceleration *
        self.esp.carriage_weight;
let target_voltage = target_force / 8.0;
if target_voltage > 0.0 {
    MotorInput::Up { voltage: target_voltage }
} else {
    MotorInput::Down { voltage: target_voltage.abs() }
}
```

```
        }
    }
```

Now, let's write a second controller, implementing the proposed improvements. We will compare the two controllers later in the simulation. The first suggestion was to reduce the polling interval. This change must be made in the physics simulator, so we will measure its effect, but we will not tie it to the motor controller. The second suggestion was to smooth the acceleration curve.

After consideration, we realized that the change in acceleration (also called **jerk**) is what made people uncomfortable, more so than small acceleration forces. Understanding this, we will permit faster acceleration so long as the jerk remains small. We will replace the current target acceleration calculation with the following constraints and objectives:

- Maximum jerk = `0.2` m/s^3
- Maximum acceleration = `2.0` m/s^2
- Maximum velocity = `5.0` m/s
- Target change in acceleration:
    - 0.2 if accelerating up
    - -0.2 if accelerating down
    - 0.0 if at stable velocity

The resulting controller becomes as follows:

```
const MAX_JERK: f64 = 0.2;
const MAX_ACCELERATION: f64 = 2.0;
const MAX_VELOCITY: f64 = 5.0;

pub struct SmoothMotorController
{
    pub esp: ElevatorSpecification,
    pub timestamp: f64
}

impl MotorController for SmoothMotorController
{
    fn init(&mut self, esp: ElevatorSpecification, est: ElevatorState)
    {
        self.esp = esp;
        self.timestamp = est.timestamp;
    }

    fn poll(&mut self, est: ElevatorState, dst: u64) -> MotorInput
    {
```

```
//5.3. Adjust motor control to process next floor request

//it will take t seconds to reach max from max
let t_accel = MAX_ACCELERATION / MAX_JERK;
let t_veloc = MAX_VELOCITY / MAX_ACCELERATION;

//it may take up to d meters to decelerate from current
let decel_t = if (est.velocity>0.0) == (est.acceleration>0.0) {
   //this case deliberately overestimates d to prevent "back up"
   (est.acceleration.abs() / MAX_JERK) +
   (est.velocity.abs() / (MAX_ACCELERATION / 2.0)) +
   2.0 * (MAX_ACCELERATION / MAX_JERK)
} else {
   //without the MAX_JERK, this approaches infinity and
      decelerates way too soon
   //MAX_JERK * 1s = acceleration in m/s^2
   est.velocity.abs() / (MAX_JERK + est.acceleration.abs())
};
let d = est.velocity.abs() * decel_t;

//l = distance to next floor
let l = (est.location - (dst as
      f64)*self.esp.floor_height).abs();
```

After determining basic constants and values, we can calculate a target acceleration:

```
let target_acceleration = {
   //are we going up?
   let going_up = est.location < (dst as
      f64)*self.esp.floor_height;

   //time elapsed since last poll
   let dt = est.timestamp - self.timestamp;
   self.timestamp = est.timestamp;

   //Do not exceed maximum acceleration
   if est.acceleration.abs() >= MAX_ACCELERATION {
      if est.acceleration > 0.0 {
         est.acceleration - (dt * MAX_JERK)
      } else {
         est.acceleration + (dt * MAX_JERK)
      }

   //Do not exceed maximum velocity
   } else if est.velocity.abs() >= MAX_VELOCITY
      || (est.velocity + est.acceleration *
         (est.acceleration.abs() / MAX_JERK)).abs() >=
               MAX_VELOCITY {
```

```
              if est.velocity > 0.0 {
                 est.acceleration - (dt * MAX_JERK)
              } else {
                 est.acceleration + (dt * MAX_JERK)
              }

          //if within comfortable deceleration range and
             moving in right direction, decelerate
          } else if l < d && (est.velocity>0.0) == going_up {
             if going_up {
                est.acceleration - (dt * MAX_JERK)
             } else {
                est.acceleration + (dt * MAX_JERK)
             }

          //else if not at peak velocity, accelerate smoothly
          } else {
             if going_up {
                est.acceleration + (dt * MAX_JERK)
             } else {
                est.acceleration - (dt * MAX_JERK)
             }
          }
       };
```

After determining a target acceleration, we should calculate a target force:

```
       let gravity_adjusted_acceleration = target_acceleration + 9.8;
       let target_force = gravity_adjusted_acceleration
             * self.esp.carriage_weight;
       let target_voltage = target_force / 8.0;
       if !target_voltage.is_finite() {
          //divide by zero etc.
          //may happen if time delta underflows
          MotorInput::Up { voltage: 0.0 }
       } else if target_voltage > 0.0 {
          MotorInput::Up { voltage: target_voltage }
       } else {
          MotorInput::Down { voltage: target_voltage.abs() }
       }
    }
 }
```

Writing the executable to run a simulation

The executable to run a simulation, contained in `src/lib.rs`, consists of all input and configuration from the previous chapter's simulation. Here is the harness used to configure and run a simulation:

```
pub fn run_simulation()
{

    //1. Store location, velocity, and acceleration state
    //2. Store motor input voltage
    let mut est = ElevatorState {
        timestamp: 0.0,
        location: 0.0,
        velocity: 0.0,
        acceleration: 0.0,
        motor_input: MotorInput::Up {
            //a positive force is required to counter gravity and
            voltage: 9.8 * (120000.0 / 8.0)
        }
    };

    //3. Store input building description and floor requests
    let mut esp = ElevatorSpecification {
        floor_count: 0,
        floor_height: 0.0,
        carriage_weight: 120000.0
    };
    let mut floor_requests = Vec::new();

    //4. Parse input and store as building description
    //        and floor requests
    let buffer = match env::args().nth(1) {
        Some(ref fp) if *fp == "-".to_string()   => {
            let mut buffer = String::new();
            io::stdin().read_to_string(&mut buffer)
                    .expect("read_to_string failed");
            buffer
        },
        None => {
            let fp = "test1.txt";
            let mut buffer = String::new();
            File::open(fp)
                .expect("File::open failed")
                .read_to_string(&mut buffer)
                .expect("read_to_string failed");
            buffer
```

```
        },
        Some(fp) => {
            let mut buffer = String::new();
            File::open(fp)
                .expect("File::open failed")
                .read_to_string(&mut buffer)
                .expect("read_to_string failed");
            buffer
        }
    };
    for (li,l) in buffer.lines().enumerate() {
        if li==0 {
            esp.floor_count = l.parse::<u64>().unwrap();
        } else if li==1 {
            esp.floor_height = l.parse::<f64>().unwrap();
        } else {
            floor_requests.push(l.parse::<u64>().unwrap());
        }
    }
}
```

After establishing the simulation state and reading the input configuration, we run the
simulation:

```
let termsize = termion::terminal_size().ok();
let mut dr = SimpleDataRecorder {
    esp: esp.clone(),
    termwidth: termsize.map(|(w,_)| w-2).expect("termwidth")
        as u64,
    termheight: termsize.map(|(_,h)| h-2).expect("termheight")
        as u64,
    stdout: &mut io::stdout().into_raw_mode().unwrap(),
    log: File::create("simulation.log").expect("log file"),
    record_location: Vec::new(),
    record_velocity: Vec::new(),
    record_acceleration: Vec::new(),
    record_voltage: Vec::new()
};
/*
let mut mc = SimpleMotorController {
    esp: esp.clone()
};
*/
let mut mc = SmoothMotorController {
    timestamp: 0.0,
    esp: esp.clone()
};

simulate_elevator(esp, est, floor_requests, &mut mc, &mut dr);
```

```
        dr.summary();

    }
```

The `DataRecorder` implementation, also in `src/lib.rs`, is responsible for outputting real-time information as well as summary information. Additionally, we will serialize and store the simulation data in a log file. Notice the use of the `lifetime` parameter along with the parameterized `trait`:

```
struct SimpleDataRecorder<'a, W: 'a + Write>
{
    esp: ElevatorSpecification,
    termwidth: u64,
    termheight: u64,
    stdout: &'a mut raw::RawTerminal<W>,
    log: File,
    record_location: Vec<f64>,
    record_velocity: Vec<f64>,
    record_acceleration: Vec<f64>,
    record_voltage: Vec<f64>,
}
impl<'a, W: Write> DataRecorder for SimpleDataRecorder<'a, W>
{
    fn init(&mut self, esp: ElevatorSpecification, est: ElevatorState)
    {
        self.esp = esp.clone();
self.log.write_all(serde_json::to_string(&esp).unwrap().as_bytes()).exp
ect("write spec to log");
        self.log.write_all(b"\r\n").expect("write spec to log");
    }
    fn poll(&mut self, est: ElevatorState, dst: u64)
    {
        let datum = (est.clone(), dst);
self.log.write_all(serde_json::to_string(&datum).unwrap().as_bytes()).e
xpect("write state to log");
        self.log.write_all(b"\r\n").expect("write state to log");

        self.record_location.push(est.location);
        self.record_velocity.push(est.velocity);
        self.record_acceleration.push(est.acceleration);
        self.record_voltage.push(est.motor_input.voltage());
```

The `DataRecorder` is responsible for not only recording simulation data to logs, but also for printing statistics to the Terminal:

```
//5.4. Print realtime statistics
print!("{}{}{}", clear::All, cursor::Goto(1, 1), cursor::Hide);
let carriage_floor = (est.location /
self.esp.floor_height).floor();
let carriage_floor = if carriage_floor < 1.0 { 0 } else {
carriage_floor as u64 };
let carriage_floor = cmp::min(carriage_floor,
self.esp.floor_count-1);
let mut terminal_buffer = vec![' ' as u8;
(self.termwidth*self.termheight) as usize];
for ty in 0..self.esp.floor_count
{
    terminal_buffer[ (ty*self.termwidth + 0) as usize ] = '[' as
u8;
    terminal_buffer[ (ty*self.termwidth + 1) as usize ] =
        if (ty as u64)==((self.esp.floor_count-1)-carriage_floor) {
'X' as u8 }
        else { ' ' as u8 };
    terminal_buffer[ (ty*self.termwidth + 2) as usize ] = ']' as
u8;
    terminal_buffer[ (ty*self.termwidth + self.termwidth-2) as
usize ] = '\r' as u8;
    terminal_buffer[ (ty*self.termwidth + self.termwidth-1) as
usize ] = '\n' as u8;
}
let stats = vec![
    format!("Carriage at floor {}", carriage_floor+1),
    format!("Location {:.06}", est.location),
    format!("Velocity {:.06}", est.velocity),
    format!("Acceleration {:.06}", est.acceleration),
    format!("Voltage [up-down] {:.06}",
est.motor_input.voltage()),
    ];
for sy in 0..stats.len()
{
    for (sx,sc) in stats[sy].chars().enumerate()
    {
        terminal_buffer[ sy*(self.termwidth as usize) + 6 + sx ] =
sc as u8;
    }
}
write!(self.stdout, "{}",
```

```
        String::from_utf8(terminal_buffer).ok().unwrap());
            self.stdout.flush().unwrap();
        }
```

The `DataRecorder` is also responsible for printing a summary at the end of the simulation:

```
        fn summary(&mut self)
        {
            //6 Calculate and print summary statistics
            write!(self.stdout, "{}{}{}", clear::All, cursor::Goto(1, 1),
    cursor::Show).unwrap();
            variable_summary(&mut self.stdout, "location".to_string(),
    &self.record_location);
            variable_summary(&mut self.stdout, "velocity".to_string(),
    &self.record_velocity);
            variable_summary(&mut self.stdout, "acceleration".to_string(),
    &self.record_acceleration);
            variable_summary(&mut self.stdout, "voltage".to_string(),
    &self.record_voltage);
            self.stdout.flush().unwrap();
        }
    }
```

Writing the executable to analyze a simulation

The analysis executable in `src/analyze.rs` should look at the log file and confirm that all requirements are satisfied—namely the following:

- Jerk is under 0.2 m/s^3
- Acceleration is under 2.0 m/s^2
- Velocity is under 5.0 m/s
- The elevator does not back up during trips
- All trips are completed within 20% of the physical theoretical limit

The program design here will be to pass through the log file and check that all values are within the specified limits. There also needs to be a directional flag to alert us to backup events. When a trip completes, we will then compare the elapsed time to the theoretical limit. If any requirement is not satisfied, we will fail immediately and print some basic information. The code is as follows:

```
#[derive(Clone)]
struct Trip {
    dst: u64,
    up: f64,
    down: f64
}

const MAX_JERK: f64 = 0.2;
const MAX_ACCELERATION: f64 = 2.0;
const MAX_VELOCITY: f64 = 5.0;

fn main()
{
    let simlog = File::open("simulation.log").expect("read simulation
log");
    let mut simlog = BufReader::new(&simlog);
    let mut jerk = 0.0;
    let mut prev_est: Option<ElevatorState> = None;
    let mut dst_timing: Vec<Trip> = Vec::new();
    let mut start_location = 0.0;
```

After initializing the analysis state, we will go through the lines in the log to calculate the statistics:

```
    let mut first_line = String::new();
    let len = simlog.read_line(&mut first_line).unwrap();
    let esp: ElevatorSpecification =
serde_json::from_str(&first_line).unwrap();

    for line in simlog.lines() {
        let l = line.unwrap();
        let (est, dst): (ElevatorState,u64) =
serde_json::from_str(&l).unwrap();
        let dl = dst_timing.len();
        if dst_timing.len()==0 || dst_timing[dl-1].dst != dst {
            dst_timing.push(Trip { dst:dst, up:0.0, down:0.0 });
        }

        if let Some(prev_est) = prev_est {
            let dt = est.timestamp - prev_est.timestamp;
            if est.velocity > 0.0 {
```

```
                    dst_timing[dl-1].up += dt;
                } else {
                    dst_timing[dl-1].down += dt;
                }
                let da = (est.acceleration - prev_est.acceleration).abs();
                jerk = (jerk * (1.0 - dt)) + (da * dt);
                if jerk.abs() > 0.22 {
                    panic!("jerk is outside of acceptable limits: {} {:?}",
jerk, est)
                }
            } else {
                start_location = est.location;
            }
            if est.acceleration.abs() > 2.2 {
                panic!("acceleration is outside of acceptable limits: {:?}",
est)
            }
            if est.velocity.abs() > 5.5 {
                panic!("velocity is outside of acceptable limits: {:?}", est)
            }
            prev_est = Some(est);
        }
```

The analysis validates some requirements as it is processing the file; other requirements must be validated only after the entire log has been processed:

```
    //elevator should not backup
    let mut total_time = 0.0;
    let mut total_direct = 0.0;
    for trip in dst_timing.clone()
    {
        total_time += (trip.up + trip.down);
        if trip.up > trip.down {
            total_direct += trip.up;
        } else {
            total_direct += trip.down;
        }
    }
    if (total_direct / total_time) < 0.9 {
        panic!("elevator back up is too common: {}", total_direct /
total_time)
    }

    //trips should finish within 20% of theoretical limit
    let mut trip_start_location = start_location;
    let mut theoretical_time = 0.0;
    let floor_height = esp.floor_height;
    for trip in dst_timing.clone()
```

```
    {
        let next_floor = (trip.dst as f64) * floor_height;
        let d = (trip_start_location - next_floor).abs();
        theoretical_time += (
            2.0*(MAX_ACCELERATION / MAX_JERK) +
            2.0*(MAX_JERK / MAX_ACCELERATION) +
            d / MAX_VELOCITY
        );
        trip_start_location = next_floor;
    }
    if total_time > (theoretical_time * 1.2) {
        panic!("elevator moves to slow {} {}", total_time,
theoretical_time * 1.2)
    }

    println!("All simulation checks passing.");
}
```

Running simulations and analyzing data

After running a simulation with SimpleMotorController, we gather an initial simulation log. A simulation log will be saved in JSON form thanks to the handy SerDe library. There should be an initial elevator specification, followed by an elevator state, for each iteration of the simulator. The simulation.log will end up looking something like the following:

```
{"floor_count":5,"floor_height":5.67,"carriage_weight":120000.0}[{"time
stamp":0.001288587,"location":0.0,"velocity":0.0,"acceleration":0.0,"mo
tor_input":{"Up":{"voltage":147000.0}}},2][{"timestamp":0.002877568,"lo
cation":0.0,"velocity":0.0,"acceleration":0.0002577174000002458,"motor_
input":{"Up":{"voltage":147003.86576100003}}},2][{"timestamp":0.0043892
54,"location":0.0,"velocity":3.8958778553677168e-7,"acceleration":0.000
575513599999411,"motor_input":{"Up":{"voltage":147008.632704}}},2][{"ti
mestamp":0.005886777,"location":5.834166693603828e-10,"velocity":0.0000
012514326383486894,"acceleration":0.0008778508000002461,"motor_input":{
"Up":{"voltage":147013.16776200004}}},2][{"timestamp":0.007377939,"loca
tion":2.449505465225691e-9,"velocity":0.0000025604503929786564,"acceler
ation":0.0011773553999994136,"motor_input":{"Up":{"voltage":147017.6603
31}}},2][{"timestamp":0.008929299,"location":6.421685786877059e-9,"velo
city":0.00000043869524663211746,"acceleration":0.0014755878000016765,"mot
or_input":{"Up":{"voltage":147022.13381700003}}},2]
```

This serialized output was created by our SerDe serialization library. There are several steps for implementing serialization using SerDe and it is very informative of how complex libraries work. To use SerDe for JSON serialization and deserialization, we must do the following:

1. Add SerDe to dependencies in `Cargo.toml` as follows:

```
[dependencies]
serde = "1.0"
serde_json = "1.0"
serde_derive = "1.0"
```

2. Add `macro_use` directives and `extern crate` imports to the project root:

```
#[macro_use] extern crate serde_derive;
extern crate serde;
extern crate serde_json;
```

3. Derive `Serialize` and `Deserialize` traits for data that will be serialized. To derive traits with macro manipulations on declarations, the `derive` directive is used. For each macro in the directive, a corresponding procedural macro is expected. Consider the following code:

```
#[derive(Clone,Serialize,Deserialize,Debug)]
pub enum MotorInput
{
    Up { voltage: f64 },
    Down { voltage: f64 }
}

#[derive(Clone,Serialize,Deserialize,Debug)]
pub struct ElevatorSpecification
{
    pub floor_count: u64,
    pub floor_height: f64,
    pub carriage_weight: f64
}

#[derive(Clone,Serialize,Deserialize,Debug)]
pub struct ElevatorState
{
    pub timestamp: f64,
    pub location: f64,
    pub velocity: f64,
```

```
        pub acceleration: f64,
        pub motor_input: MotorInput
    }
```

4. Serialize data as needed. In `lib.rs`, we serialize `ElevatorSpecification` and `ElevatorState` structs. Type hints are often necessary, as the type system doesn't like guessing:

```
    serde_json::to_string(&datum).unwrap().as_bytes()
```

5. Deserialize data as needed. In `analyze.rs`, we deserialize lines into `ElevatorSpecification` and `ElevatorState` structs. Type hints are often necessary, as the type system doesn't like guessing:

```
    serde_json::from_str(&l).unwrap()
```

SerDe supports many built-in types to serialize and deserialize. These roughly correspond to all types that JSON permits, with additional structs permitted through type hints.

Looking through `simulation.log`, we can find most of the built-in types:

- **Integer types**: Integer types become direct JSON integers:

  ```
      5
  ```

- **Floating point types**: Floating point integers become direct JSON floats:

  ```
      6.54321
  ```

- **Strings**: Rust strings are also translated directly into JSON equivalents:

  ```
      "timestamp"
  ```

- **Vectors and arrays**: Rust collections are sometimes serialized in unexpected ways. For the most part, vector types are translated directly into JSON arrays; containing the serialized version of whatever the vector contains:

  ```
      [1,2,3,4,5,6,0]
  ```

- **Tuples**: Tuples are serialized into JSON arrays, however, the compiler typically requires a type hint to understand how to serialize/deserialize these types:

```
[{"timestamp":0.007377939,"location":2.449505465225691e-9,"velocity
":0.0000025604503929786564,"acceleration":0.0011773553999994136,"mo
tor_input":{"Up":{"voltage":147017.660331}}},2][{"timestamp":0.0089
29299,"location":6.421685786877059e-9,"velocity":0.0000043869524663
21746,"acceleration":0.0014755878000016765,"motor_input":{"Up":{"vo
ltage":147022.13381700003}}},2]
```

- **Structs**: Rust structs are translated directly into JSON objects. This always succeeds because Rust field names are valid object keys, as follows:

```
{"floor_count":5,"floor_height":5.67,"carriage_weight":120000.0}
```

- **Tagged unions**: Tagged unions are a slightly strange case. The union constructor is converted into a JSON object like any other struct. The union tag, however, is also given its own struct, wrapping the union constructor in a separate object. Type hints are very much necessary for the compiler to serialize/deserialize correctly here:

```
{"Up":{"voltage":147003.86576100003}}
```

- **HashMap**: Rust HashMaps are an odd case for serialization. The library attempts to convert them to JSON objects. However, not all HashMap keys can be serialized. Therefore, some serialization may fail and require custom serializers:

```
{"a":5,"b":6,"c":7}
```

Some types are difficult to serialize, including time structures such as `Instant`. Despite this difficulty in processing certain datatypes, the SerDe library is very stable, fast, and indispensable when storing and loading data.

Running the analysis program, we can confirm that this motor controller is insufficient for meeting current project requirements:

```
jerk is outside of acceptable limits: ElevatorState {
    timestamp: 0.023739637,
    location: 0,
    velocity: 0,
    acceleration: 1,
    motor_input: Up { voltage: 162000 }
}
```

Switching to `SmoothMotorController`, we can see that all specifications are met:

```
All simulation checks passing.
```

Summary

In this chapter, we outlined the steps to address changes to the project scope and new specifications. We focused on how to write robust code that will encourage reuse in further additional projects or refinements.

Using a wide variety of data structures helps to organize our project and data. The code should be self-documenting whenever possible. Additionally, typesafe code can enforce some assumptions about code to block incorrect input and inappropriate usage. Through the use of data classes, we also learned how to extend existing data structures to support new uses. We also used data classes as an interface to defer assumptions about project elements that were uncertain.

In the next chapter, we will learn about parameterization and generics. We will perform an in-depth code review along with case analysis.

Questions

1. What is a good library to serialize and deserialize data?
2. What do the hashtag derive lines in front of the struct declarations in `physics.rs` do?
3. Which comes first in parameterized declarations—lifetimes or traits?
4. In a `trait` implementation, what is the difference between parameters on the `impl`, `trait`, or `type`?
5. What is the difference between a `trait` and a data class?
6. How should you declare that a package has multiple binaries?
7. How do you declare a structure field as private?

4
Generics and Polymorphism

Parameterization, also known as **generics** or **polymorphism**, is the third most significant language feature following control flow and data structures. Parameterization addresses the copy-and-paste problem of early languages. This feature permits the *don't repeat yourself* principle of good program design.

In this chapter, we will look at how parameterization can help us design robust programs that evolve with change rather than fight against change. No new project requirements will be introduced. This chapter will be entirely reflective, looking at how the project is currently structured, how can it be improved, and how parameterization can specifically help.

The following are the learning outcomes of this chapter:

- Understanding generalized algebraic datatypes
- Understanding parametric polymorphism
- Understanding parametric lifetimes
- Understanding parametric traits
- Understanding ambiguous method resolution

Technical requirements

A recent version of Rust is necessary to run the examples provided:

```
https://www.rust-lang.org/en-US/install.html
```

This chapter's code is also available on GitHub:

```
https://github.com/PacktPublishing/Hands-On-Functional-Programming-in-RUST
```

Specific installation and build instructions are also included in each chapter's README.md file.

Staying productive during downtime

There will be some time before the client makes a final decision regarding negotiation and potential acceptance of your project proposal. During that time, your management has encouraged you to take this time to review your work and make preparations for integrating the elevator controller into a real elevator.

You do not know much about direct elevator control interfaces, and the client specifically mentioned that there may be multiple subcontractors designing each of the different elevators. Making assumptions at this point may lead to wasted effort so, instead, you decide to reconsider your code and look for opportunities to remove any assumptions.

Parameterization and use of trait interfaces should help achieve this goal of abstraction. During this downtime, you decide to have the team learn about parameterization and consider how it can be applied to improve this project or later projects.

Learning about generics

Generics are a facility to write code for multiple contexts with different types, and parameterization allows the programmer to write code that makes fewer assumptions about the data structures and code segments involved in the code's definition. For example, a very ambiguous concept would be the concept of addition. When a programmer writes `a + b`, what does that mean? In Rust, the `Add` trait can be implemented for just about any type. As long as there is an implementation for the `Add` trait in scope that is compatible with the types of `a` and `b`, then this trait will define the operation. In this pattern, we can write generic code that defines a concept in its most abstract terms, allowing for later definitions of data and methods to interface with that code without change.

A major example of completely generic code are built-in container data structures. Vectors and HashMaps must necessarily know the types of the objects they store. However, it would be very limiting if any assumptions were made about the underlying data structure or methods for the stored items. Therefore, parameterization of containers allows the container and its methods to explicitly declare trait bounds that are expected from stored types. All other characteristics of the stored item will be parameterized.

Investigating generics

Generics refers to the practice of parameterizing classes in object-oriented programming languages. Rust does not have an exact equivalent of classes. However, the concept of datatypes paired with a trait is very similar to a class if used in that sense. So, in Rust, generics would refer to the parameterization of datatypes and traits.

Choosing a common example from OOP, let's look at the animal kingdom. In the following code, we will define some animals and actions that they can take. First, let's define two animals:

```rust
struct Cat
{
    weight: f64,
    speed: f64
}

struct Dog
{
    weight: f64,
    speed: f64
}
```

Now, let's define an `animal trait` and its implementations. All animals will have the `max_speed` method. Here is the code:

```rust
trait Animal
{
    fn max_speed(&self) -> f64;
}

impl Animal for Cat
{
    fn max_speed(&self) -> f64
    {
        self.speed
    }
}

impl Animal for Dog
{
    fn max_speed(&self) -> f64
    {
        self.speed
    }
}
```

Here, we have defined the Rust equivalent of interfaces from OOP. However, we have not parameterized anything, so nothing here should be considered generic. We will add the following code, a trait defining the concept of an animal chasing a toy. First, we will define the concept of a toy. This will follow the same OOP-like pattern as in the preceding code:

```
struct SqueakyToy
{
    weight: f64
}

struct Stick
{
    weight: f64
}

trait Toy
{
    fn weight(&self) -> f64;
}

impl Toy for SqueakyToy
{
    fn weight(&self) -> f64
    {
        self.weight
    }
}

impl Toy for Stick
{
    fn weight(&self) -> f64
    {
        self.weight
    }
}
```

Now, we have two traits, each having two possible implementations. Let's define an action for an animal chasing a toy. More than one possible animal has been defined, and more than one possible toy, so we will need to use a generic definition. The struct definition also constrains each parameter with a trait bound, which adds additional information to the struct; now, we can guarantee that each animal will implement the Animal trait and similarly, each toy will implement Toy. We will also define some associated logic that uses the parameterized traits' methods. The code is as follows:

```
struct AnimalChasingToy<A: Animal, T: Toy>
{
    animal: A,
    toy: T
}

trait AnimalChasesToy<A: Animal, T: Toy>
{
    fn chase(&self);
}

impl<A: Animal, T: Toy> AnimalChasesToy<A, T> for AnimalChasingToy<A,
T>
{
    fn chase(&self)
    {
        println!("chase")
    }
}
```

At this point, we have defined a generic `struct` and `trait` that accepts types, knowing only some limited information regarding the traits of each object. Multiple traits, or none, can be specified to declare all expected interfaces. Multiple traits or lifetime bounds can be declared with the `'1 + Trait1 + Trait2` syntax.

Investigating parametric polymorphism

Another common application of parameterization are for functions. For the same reasons that we would want to parameterize data structures or traits, we also should consider parameterization of functions. Parameterizing functions is called **parametric polymorphism**. Polymorphism is Greek for multiple forms or, sometimes in modern usage, it can mean multiple arrows. The word indicates that one function has multiple implementations or multiple ground type signatures.

For a simple example of a parametric function, we can imagine a generic multiply by three function. Here is the implementation:

```
fn raise_by_three<T: Mul + Copy>(x: T) -> T
where T: std::ops::Mul<Output=T>
{
    x * x * x
}
```

Here, the `raise_by_three` function does not know what `Mul` does. `Mul` is a trait and abstract behavior, which also specifies an associated type, `Output`. It is not possible to generically raise `x.pow(3)` here because `x` may not be a numerical type. At the very least, we do not know whether `x` is a floating type or an integral type. So instead, we use the available `Mul` trait to multiply `x` three times. This may seem like a strange thing to do, but the concept becomes clearer in context.

First, consider the application in regard to floating and integral types. This usage is straightforward but does not seem very useful yet. We already have a working `raise by three` expression, as long as we know and have the original floating or integral type. So, why wouldn't we just use the built-in expression? First, let's just compare the two options in code:

```
raise_by_three(10);
(10 as u64).pow(3);

raise_by_three(3.0);
(3.0 as f64).powi(3);
```

The second option seems much more preferable, and it is. However, the second option also assumes we know the full type of `u64` or `f64` for each argument. Let's look at what happens if we erase some type information:

```
#[derive(Copy,Clone)]
struct Raiseable<T: Mul + Copy>
{
    x: T
}

impl<T: Mul + Copy> std::ops::Mul for Raiseable<T>
where T: std::ops::Mul<Output=T>
{
    type Output = Raiseable<T>;
    fn mul(self, rhs: Self) -> Self::Output
    {
        Raiseable { x: self.x * rhs.x }
    }
}

let x = Raiseable { x: 10 as u64 };
raise_by_three(x);
//no method named pow
//x.pow(3);
```

```
let x = Raiseable { x: 3.0 as f64 };
raise_by_three(x);
//no method named powi
//x.powi(3);
```

After we lose access to the underlying types, we are quickly restricted in regard to what operations we can perform. Generic programming is great in the respect that it can reduce work in the long term; however, it also requires very explicit declaration and implementation of all interfaces that are used. Here, you can see that we must declare Copy as a trait bound, meaning the ability to copy a variable from one memory location to another. Another low-level trait is Sized, which indicates that a datum has a known constant size at compile time.

If we look at the HashMap declaration, we can see why this abstraction is often necessary:

```
impl<K: Hash + Eq, V> HashMap<K, V, RandomState>
```

Each hash key must implement Hash and Eq, meaning it must be hashable and comparable. Other than that, no traits are expected and thus the whole data structure remains very generic.

Just as functions can be parameterized, functions as arguments can also be parameterized. There are two general forms of functions as parameters—closures and function pointers. Function pointers are not permitted to carry state. Closures can carry state but have a variable size which is independent of their declared type. Function pointers can be promoted to closures automatically:

```
fn foo<X>(x: X) -> X
{
    x
}

fn bar<X>(f: fn(X) -> X, x: X) -> X
{
    f(x)
}

foo(1);
bar(foo,1);
```

Closures can also be parameterized in a similar fashion. This case is a bit more common. If you are wondering whether to use a function pointer or a closure, use the closure. Function pointers can always be promoted to closures. Also, this code introduces the `where` syntax; `where` clauses permit trait bounds to be declared in a more readable form. Here is the code:

```
fn baz<X,F>(f: F, x: X) -> X
where F: Fn(X) -> X
{
    f(x)
}

baz(|x| x, 1);
baz(foo, 1);
```

Here, we can see how easy it is to wrap a function pointer into a closure. Closures are a good abstraction and very powerful when used correctly.

Investigating generalized algebraic datatypes

Sometimes, it is desirable to have the type system carry more information than normal. If we look at the process of compilation, types occupy a space between the program code and the program executable. The code can take the form of text files before compilation or an abstract syntax tree such as those manipulated by Rust macros. Program executables consist of the resulting combination of all Rust primitives like expressions, functions, datatypes, traits, and so on.

Right in the middle, it is possible to introduce a new concept called **algebraic data types** (**ADTs**). ADTs are technically an extension of Rust primitives, though it is important to note how much extra type information is used for ADTs. This technique involves preserving extra type information into the executable. Extra run time decision-making is a step towards dynamic typing and foregoes optimizations available to static compilation. The result is a somewhat less efficient programming primitive, but also a primitive that can describe concepts that are otherwise difficult to approach.

Let's look at one example—deferred computation. When we describe a relation of different values and expressions, we normally just write this code into the program directly. However, what would we do if we wanted to separate the code step from the execution step? To accomplish this, we start building something called a **domain-specific language**.

For a concrete example, consider that you are building a JIT (dynamically compiled) interpreter for JavaScript. The Mozilla project has several projects dedicated to JS engines built in Rust (https://blog.mozilla.org/javascript/2017/10/20/holyjit-a-new-hope/). This is a real application for which Rust is well-suited. To use an ADT in a JIT compiled interpreter, we want two things:

- To evaluate ADT expressions directly within the interpreter
- To compile ADT expressions if selected for compilation

So, any part of our JavaScript expressions can either be interpreted or compiled at any time. If an expression is compiled, then we want all further evaluations to use the compiled version. The key to implementing this cleanly is to put some extra weight on the type system. These heavy type definitions are the essence of the ADT concept. Here is a definition of a very small subset of JavaScript using an ADT:

```
struct JSJIT(u64);

enum JSJITorExpr {
    Jit { label: Box<JSJIT> },
    Expr { expr: Box<JSExpr> }
}

enum JSExpr {
    Integer { value: u64 },
    String { value: String },
    OperatorAdd { lexpr: Box<JSJITorExpr>, rexpr: Box<JSJITorExpr> },
    OperatorMul { lexpr: Box<JSJITorExpr>, rexpr: Box<JSJITorExpr> }
}
```

Here, we can see that each intermediate expression has enough information to be evaluated, but also has enough information to be compiled. We could have easily wrapped the Add or Mul operator into closures, but that would disallow JIT optimization. We need to maintain the full representation here in order to permit JIT compilation. Also, note the indirection between each point where the program decides whether to evaluate an expression or to call into compiled code.

The next step is to implement an evaluation program for each expression form. We could break this into traits, or define the evaluation as one larger function. To keep the functional style, we will define a single function. To evaluate an expression, we will use a pattern match on the `JSJITorExpr` expression. This JIT expression breaks down into either a code address which is run by calling the `jump` function or an expression which must be evaluated dynamically. This pattern gives us the best of both worlds, mixing compiled code and interpreted code together. The code is as follows:

```
fn jump(l: JSJIT) -> JSJITorExpr
{
    //jump to compiled code
    //this depends on implementation
    //so we will just leave this as a stub
    JSJITorExpr::Jit { label: JSJIT(0) }
}

fn eval(e: JSJITorExpr) -> JSJITorExpr
{
    match e
    {
        JSJITorExpr::Jit { label: label } => jump(label),
        JSJITorExpr::Expr { expr: expr } => {
            let rawexpr = *expr;
            match rawexpr
            {
                JSExpr::Integer {..} => JSJITorExpr::Expr { expr:
Box::new(rawexpr) },
                JSExpr::String {..} => JSJITorExpr::Expr { expr:
Box::new(rawexpr) },
                JSExpr::OperatorAdd { lexpr: l, rexpr: r } => {
                    let l = eval(*l);
                    let r = eval(*r);
                    //call add op codes for possible l,r representations
                    //should return wrapped value from above
                    JSJITorExpr::Jit { label: JSJIT(0) }
                }
                JSExpr::OperatorMul { lexpr: l, rexpr: r } => {
                    let l = eval(*l);
                    let r = eval(*r);
                    //call mul op codes for possible l,r representations
                    //should return wrapped value from above
                    JSJITorExpr::Jit { label: JSJIT(0) }
                }
            }
        }
    }
}
```

```
        }
```

Another example of the ADT concept is in heterogeneous lists. Heterogeneous lists are not like other generic containers, such as vectors. Rust vectors are homogeneous, meaning all items are required to have the same type. By comparison, a heterogeneous list can have any mix of types of elements. This may sound like a tuple, but tuples have a fixed length and flat type signature. Similarly, heterogeneous lists must have a length and type signature known at compile time, but that knowledge can be achieved incrementally. Heterogeneous lists are permitted to work with partial knowledge of the list type, parameterizing the knowledge that they do not need.

Here is an example implementation of a heterogeneous list:

```
pub trait HList: Sized {}

pub struct HNil;
impl HList for HNil {}

pub struct HCons<H, T> {
    pub head: H,
    pub tail: T,
}
impl<H, T: HList> HList for HCons<H, T> {}
impl<H, T> HCons<H, T> {
    pub fn pop(self) -> (H, T) {
        (self.head, self.tail)
    }
}
```

Notice how this definition intentionally uses a trait to obscure type information, without which, such a definition would be impossible. A declaration of an `HList` would look like the following:

```
let hl = HCons {
    head: 2,
    tail: HCons {
        head: "abcd".to_string(),
        tail: HNil
    }
};

let (h1,t1) = hl.pop();
let (h2,t2) = t1.pop();
//this would fail
//HNil has no .pop method
//t2.pop();
```

Rust can be a bit rigid with regards to type checking, at times. However, there are also many workarounds that permit complex behavior that might seem impossible at first.

Investigating parametric lifetimes

Lifetimes can get complicated quickly. For example, when a lifetime is used as a parameter, it is called a **parametric lifetime**. To cover the most common problems, we will break down the lifetime concept into four distinct concepts:

- Lifetimes on ground types
- Lifetimes on generic types
- Lifetimes on traits
- Lifetime subtyping

Defining lifetimes on ground types

A ground type is a type with no parameters. Defining lifetimes on ground types is the simplest possible case. All traits, fields, size, and any other information is directly available for group types.

Here is a function declaring a lifetime on a ground type:

```
fn ground_lifetime<'a>(x: &'a u64) -> &'a u64
{
    x
}

let x = 3;
ground_lifetime(&x);
```

Declaring lifetimes is often unnecessary. Other times, declaring lifetimes is necessary. The inference rules are complicated and are sometimes extended, so we will ignore that part for now.

Defining lifetimes on generic types

Declaring lifetimes on generic types requires one additional consideration. All generic types that have a specified lifetime must be parameterized as having that lifetime. The parameter declaration must be compatible with how the parameter is used.

Here is an example that will fail:

```
struct Ref<'a, T>(&'a T);
```

The struct definition uses the parameter T having a lifetime of 'a; however, the parameter T is not required to have a lifetime compatible with 'a. The parameter T must be constrained by its own lifetime. By doing this, the code becomes as follows:

```
struct Ref<'a, T: 'a>(&'a T);
```

Now that the parameter T has an explicit bound compatible with 'a, the code will compile.

Defining lifetimes on traits

When defining, implementing, and instantiating an object implementing a trait, it is possible that both the object and trait will require a lifetime. Usually, it is possible to infer the lifetime of the trait from the lifetime of the object. When this is not possible, the programmer must declare a lifetime for the trait, which is compatible with all other constraints. The code is as follows:

```
trait Red { }

struct Ball<'a> {
    diameter: &'a i32,
}

impl<'a> Red for Ball<'a> { }

static num: i32 = 5;
let obj = Box::new(Ball { diameter: &num }) as Box<Red + 'static>;
```

Defining lifetime subtyping

It is possible to have a single object that requires a long lifetime for itself but also needs a shorter lifetime for some of its components or methods. This can be accomplished by parameterizing multiple lifetimes. This usually works well unless the lifetimes come into conflict. The following is an example of multiple lifetimes:

```
struct Context<'s>(&'s mut String);

impl<'s> Context<'s>
{
    fn mutate<'c>(&mut self, cs: &'c mut String) -> &'c mut String
```

```
    {
        let swap_a = self.0.pop().unwrap();
        let swap_b = cs.pop().unwrap();
        self.0.push(swap_b);
        cs.push(swap_a);
        cs
    }
}

fn main() {
    let mut s = "outside string context abc".to_string();
    {
        //temporary context
        let mut c = Context(&mut s);
        {
            //further temporary context
            let mut s2 = "inside string context def".to_string();
            c.mutate(&mut s2);
            println!("s2 {}", s2);
        }
    }
    println!("s {}", s);
}
```

Investigating parametric types

At this point, it shouldn't be surprising to learn that all datatype declarations can be parameterized. It should be noted that when declaring parameterized datatypes, the lifetime parameters must be located ahead of the generic parameters. Refer to the following code for this:

```
type TFoo<'a, A: 'a> = (&'a A, u64);

struct SFoo<'a, A: 'a>(&'a A);

struct SBar<'a, A: 'a>
{
    x: &'a A
}

enum EFoo<'a, A: 'a>
{
    X { x: &'a A },
    Y { y: &'a A },
```

```
}
```

We have also seen how traits can be parameterized. However, what happens when a datatype and a trait both need parameters for implementation? There is a special syntax for that, involving three parameter lists, and it looks like the following:

```
struct SBaz<'a, 'b, A: 'a, B: 'b>
{
    a: &'a A,
    b: &'b B,
}

trait TBaz<'a, 'b, A: 'a, B: 'b>
{
    fn baz(&self);
}

impl<'a, 'b, A: 'a, B: 'b>
TBaz<'a, 'b, A, B>
for SBaz<'a, 'b, A, B>
{
    fn baz(&self){}
}
```

There is one more special case that we should mention, and that is the case of method ambiguity. When multiple traits are implemented for a single type, it is possible for there to be multiple methods with the same name. To access the different methods, it becomes necessary to specify what trait is intended to be used when called. Here is an example:

```
trait Foo {
    fn f(&self);
}

trait Bar {
    fn f(&self);
}

struct Baz;

impl Foo for Baz {
    fn f(&self) { println!("Baz's impl of Foo"); }
}

impl Bar for Baz {
    fn f(&self) { println!("Baz's impl of Bar"); }
}
```

```
let b = Baz;
```

To call the method, we must use something called the **universal function call syntax**. There are two forms of the syntax, one short—the other longer. The short form is usually sufficient for resolving all but the most complicated of situations. Here is an example to match the preceding type definitions:

```
Foo::f(&b);
Bar::f(&b);

<Baz as Foo>::f(&b);
<Baz as Bar>::f(&b);
```

There are also several less documented syntax forms (https://matematikaadit.github.io/posts/rust-turbofish.html) syntax forms available for various scenarios where parameters need to be explicitly provided. Rust does not currently have direct type ascription currently, so hints for the compiler are provided as necessary.

Applying parameterization concepts

We have explored the concepts of generics and parameterization. Let's scan through the project to see if any concepts would be appropriate to use.

Parameterizing data

Parametric data allows us to declare only the minimal amount of semantic information required. Instead of specifying a type, we can specify a generic parameter having a trait. Let's start by looking at physics.rs type declarations:

```
#[derive(Clone,Serialize,Deserialize,Debug)]
pub enum MotorInput
{
    Up { voltage: f64 },
    Down { voltage: f64 }
}

#[derive(Clone,Serialize,Deserialize,Debug)]
pub struct ElevatorSpecification
{
    pub floor_count: u64,
    pub floor_height: f64,
```

```
    pub carriage_weight: f64
}
#[derive(Clone,Serialize,Deserialize,Debug)]
pub struct ElevatorState
{
    pub timestamp: f64,
    pub location: f64,
    pub velocity: f64,
    pub acceleration: f64,
    pub motor_input: MotorInput
}

pub type FloorRequests = Vec<u64>;
```

If we remember, where we used `physics.rs` when we designed the new `MotorInput`
implementation, we should notice a problem. We wanted to abstract `MotorInput` behavior
behind a trait; however, `ElevatorState` specifies a specific implementation. Let's redefine
`ElevatorState` to use a generic type for `motor_input`. The parameter should implement
all traits of `MotorInput`, and will, therefore, become as follows:

```
#[derive(Clone,Serialize,Deserialize,Debug)]
pub struct ElevatorState<MI: MotorForce + MotorVoltage + Clone, 'a
serde::Serialize, 'a serde::Deserialize + Debug>
{
    pub timestamp: f64,
    pub location: f64,
    pub velocity: f64,
    pub acceleration: f64,
    pub motor_input: MI
}
```

This may look acceptable at first glance, but now the `MotorInput` parameter and all traits
must be declared along with every mention of any type that wraps `MotorInput` or
`ElevatorState`. We get an explosion of parameters. There must be a better way.

Parameter explosion, in this case, would look like the following, at every type declaration,
trait declaration, implementation, function, or expression:

```
pub trait MotorController
<MI: MotorForce + MotorVoltage + Clone, 'a serde::Serialize, 'a
serde::Deserialize + Debug>
{
    fn init(&mut self, esp: ElevatorSpecification, est:
ElevatorState<MI>);
    fn poll(&mut self, est: ElevatorState<MI>, dst: u64) -> MI;
```

```
}

pub trait DataRecorder
<MI: MotorForce + MotorVoltage + Clone, 'a serde::Serialize, 'a
serde::Deserialize + Debug>
{
    fn init(&mut self, esp: ElevatorSpecification, est:
ElevatorState<MI>);
    fn poll(&mut self, est: ElevatorState<MI>, dst: u64);
}

impl MotorController
<MI: MotorForce + MotorVoltage + Clone, 'a serde::Serialize, 'a
serde::Deserialize + Debug>
for SimpleMotorController
<MI: MotorForce + MotorVoltage + Clone, 'a serde::Serialize, 'a
serde::Deserialize + Debug>
{
    ...
}
```

This is all just for one parameter! Fortunately, there is another solution to this problem. The technique uses something called **trait objects**. A trait object is an object implementing a trait but having no known type at compile time. Trait objects, because they have no concrete type, do not need to be parameterized. The downside of trait objects are that they cannot be sized, and therefore must usually be handled indirectly through a Box or some other sized container. Any attempt to size a trait object will result in a compiler error. Similarly, any trait that has a static method, or is otherwise not object-safe, cannot be used with a trait object.

We can rewrite the `MotorInput` and `ElevatorState` objects to use trait objects as follows:

```
#[derive(Clone,Serialize,Deserialize,Debug)]
pub enum SimpleMotorInput
{
    Up { voltage: f64 },
    Down { voltage: f64 }
}

pub trait MotorInput: MotorForce + MotorVoltage
{
}
```

```
impl MotorInput for SimpleMotorInput {}
pub struct ElevatorState
{
    pub timestamp: f64,
    pub location: f64,
    pub velocity: f64,
    pub acceleration: f64,
    pub motor_input: Box<MotorInput>
}
```

Here, we declare that a MotorInput trait has two subtraits specifying the behavior. Our ElevatorState declaration does not require a parameter; however, the MotorInput trait object must be wrapped in a Box. This layer of indirection is required due to the inability of the compiler to size the MotorInput trait object for compilation. Also, because MotorInput does not implement Sized, it cannot use the Clone or serde macros. Some of our code needs to be changed to accommodate this, but it is not overwhelming.

Parameterizing functions and trait objects

In our motor controllers, we make another baseless assumption about the motor. Namely, that a flat force will be generated per voltage input. The suspect code in the motor controllers looks like the following:

```
let target_voltage = target_force / 8.0;
```

The assumption may be wrong with respect to the motor being more or less efficient than assumed. Also, the assumption that generated force will be linear with respect to voltage is unlikely. To satisfy the requirements of our motor controller and the physics simulation, we require one function that will consider the physical motor being used and convert the voltage to force. Similarly, we need the inverse function to convert the target force to target voltage. We can write these plainly as follows:

```
pub fn force_of_voltage(v: f64) -> f64
{
    8.0 * v
}

pub fn voltage_of_force(v: f64) -> f64
{
    v / 8.0
}
```

This is nice to look at, but it doesn't fit into the goal of abstracting the concept of a physical motor. We should define these functions as methods on an interface. This way, we can use the trait object pattern again to abstract away the type of motor, as well as the type parameter for the motor. The code becomes as follows:

```
pub trait Motor
{
    fn force_of_voltage(&self, v: f64) -> f64;
    fn voltage_of_force(&self, v: f64) -> f64;
}

pub struct SimpleMotor;
impl Motor for SimpleMotor
{
    fn force_of_voltage(&self, v: f64) -> f64
    {
        8.0 * v
    }
    fn voltage_of_force(&self, v: f64) -> f64
    {
        v / 8.0
    }
}
```

After declaring the Motor trait and an implementation, we can integrate this definition with the ElevatorSpecification struct. The result is as follows:

```
pub struct ElevatorSpecification
{
    pub floor_count: u64,
    pub floor_height: f64,
    pub carriage_weight: f64,
    pub motor: Box<Motor>
}
```

Again, we lose the ability to use certain derive macros, but the type signature is much cleaner at least. The usage in the motor controllers now supports multiple motors:

```
let target_voltage = self.esp.motor.voltage_of_force(target_force);
```

We can see that there are some potential tradeoffs between different types of parameterization or generic behavior. On one hand, parameters can quickly become overwhelming to keep track of. On the other, side trait objects break many languages with features such as derive macros, anything that is not object-safe, requiring a concrete type, and so on. Choosing the right tool is an important decision that requires weighing the merits of each option.

Parametric traits and implementations

Now, we have successfully implemented `Motor` and `MotorInput` as trait objects. However, we sacrificed nice things like `Clone`, `Serialize`, `Deserialize`, and `Debug` to accomplish this. Can we reclaim those functionalities?

First, let's try to duplicate the functionality. We will call these bundled traits `ElevatorStateClone` and `ElevatorSpecificationClone`. The signatures should look something like the following (the trait implementations are available in the `src/physics.rs` file):

```
pub trait ElevatorStateClone
{
    fn clone(&self) -> ElevatorState;
    fn dump(&self) -> (f64,f64,f64,f64,f64);
    fn load((f64,f64,f64,f64,f64)) -> ElevatorState;
}

pub trait ElevatorSpecificationClone
{
    fn clone(&self) -> ElevatorSpecification;
    fn dump(&self) -> (u64,f64,f64,u64);
    fn load((u64,f64,f64,u64)) -> ElevatorSpecification;
}

impl ElevatorStateClone for ElevatorState {
    ...
}
```

These traits provide the bare minimum functionality to get us back to where we were previously with serialization and copy semantics. The major downside is that each definition is quite verbose. Additionally, the serialization turns into a tuple, rather than going directly back and forth between the correct type.

So, what precisely is the problem with trait objects? We know that they must be wrapped in `Box` types to circumvent the unknown size. Is this the problem? Here is a program to test this theory:

```
#[derive(Serialize,Deserialize)]
struct Foo
{
    bar: Box<u64>
}
```

So, `Box` types can be serialized. The problem, then, must be with the trait object. Let's try the same thing with a trait object to see what happens:

```
trait T {}

#[derive(Serialize,Deserialize)]
struct S1;
impl T for S1 {}

#[derive(Serialize,Deserialize)]
struct S2;
impl T for S2 {}

#[derive(Serialize,Deserialize)]
struct Container
{
    field: Box<T>
}
```

When compiling this last snippet, we get the error, `the trait 'serde::Deserialize<'_>' is not implemented for 'T'`. So, we can see that the individual structs `S1` and `S2` both implement `Deserialize`, but that information is obscured. The trait object `T` itself must implement `Deserialize`.

Making the first attempt at serializing the trait object `T`, we can follow the instructions for writing custom serialization. The result should be something like the following:

```
impl Serialize for Box<T>
{
    fn serialize<S>(&self, serializer: S) -> Result<S::Ok, S::Error>
    where S: Serializer
    {
        serializer.serialize_unit_struct("S1")
    }
}

struct S1Visitor;
impl<'de> Visitor<'de> for S1Visitor {
    type Value = Box<T>;

    fn expecting(&self, formatter: &mut fmt::Formatter) -> fmt::Result
    {
        formatter.write_str("an S1 structure")
    }
    fn visit_unit<E>(self) -> Result<Self::Value, E>
    where E: de::Error
```

```
    {
        Result::Ok(Box::new(S1))
    }
}

impl<'de> Deserialize<'de> for Box<T> {
    fn deserialize<D>(deserializer: D) -> Result<Box<T>, D::Error>
    where D: Deserializer<'de>
    {
        deserializer.deserialize_unit_struct("S1", S1Visitor)
    }
}

let bt: Box<T> = Box::new(S1);
let s = serde_json::to_string(&bt).unwrap();
let bt: Box<T> = serde_json::from_str(s.as_str()).unwrap();
```

This is a bit of a mess, but the important parts are that we want to write S1 or S2 to the serializer and check for those tags to deserialize. Essentially, what we are trying to create is a side enum to exist just for the purpose of serialization. Somehow, the serializer needs to know whether T is an S1 or S2 through the interface, so why not, in turn, provide a method on T that will return an enum? Enums are also serializable with macros, so we could pass that automatic serialization through to T. Let's try that, starting with the type and trait definitions, as follows:

```
#[derive(Clone,Serialize,Deserialize)]
enum T_Enum
{
    S1(S1),
    S2(S2),
}

trait T
{
    fn as_enum(&self) -> T_Enum;
}

#[derive(Clone,Serialize,Deserialize)]
struct S1;
impl T for S1
{
    fn as_enum(&self) -> T_Enum
    {
        T_Enum::S1(self.clone())
    }
}
```

```
}
#[derive(Clone,Serialize,Deserialize)]
struct S2;
impl T for S2
{
    fn as_enum(&self) -> T_Enum
    {
        T_Enum::S2(self.clone())
    }
}
```

Here, we can see that there is no issue in permitting a method on a trait object that turns the object into an enum. This relation is natural and provides an escape hatch to convert back and forth between the trait objects and its internal representation. Now, to implement serialization, we just need to wrap and unwrap the enum serializers:

```
impl Serialize for Box<T>
{
    fn serialize<S>(&self, serializer: S) -> Result<S::Ok, S::Error>
    where S: Serializer
    {
        self.as_enum().serialize(serializer)
    }
}

impl<'de> Deserialize<'de> for Box<T>
{
    fn deserialize<D>(deserializer: D) -> Result<Box<T>, D::Error>
    where D: Deserializer<'de>
    {
        let result = T_Enum::deserialize(deserializer);
        match result
        {
            Result::Ok(te) => {
                match te {
                    T_Enum::S1(s1) => Result::Ok(Box::new(s1.clone())),
                    T_Enum::S2(s2) => Result::Ok(Box::new(s2.clone()))
                }
            }
            Result::Err(err) => Result::Err(err)
        }
    }
}
```

That wasn't so bad, was it? With this technique, we can hide parameters behind trait objects while still benefiting from the direct access to data and macro-derived traits. There is a little bit of boilerplate here. Luckily though, for each macro, the code is almost identical for whatever type you are using. Remember this one; it could be useful.

Summary

In this chapter, we explored the basic and deeper concepts of generic and parameterized programming. We learned how to add lifetime, type, and trait parameters to declarations of types, traits, functions, and implementations. We also examined advanced techniques to selectively preserve or obscure type information as desired.

Applying these concepts to the elevator simulation, we observed how parameterization and generics can create fully abstract interfaces. By using trait objects, it is possible to completely separate trait interfaces from any implementation. We also observed the downsides or difficulties of parameterization and generics. Excessive use of parameterization can lead to parameter leaks, potentially requiring all code that interfaces with an interface to also become parameterized itself. On the other hand, we observed the difficulty associated with erasing type information using trait objects. Choosing the right amount of information to preserve is important.

In the next chapter, we will learn about applied project structure with complex requirements. The client will respond to the project proposal and your team will respond to new requirements.

Questions

1. What is an algebraic datatype?
2. What is polymorphism?
3. What is parametric polymorphism?
4. What is a ground type?
5. What is universal function call syntax?
6. What are the possible type signatures of a trait object?
7. What are two ways to obscure type information?
8. How is a subtrait declared?

5
Code Organization and Application Architecture

Previously, we outlined some basic concepts of project planning and code architecture. The strategy we recommended specifically called for gathering and listing requirements before adapting them into pseudocode, stub code, and eventually a completed project. This process is still very applicable to larger projects, but we have not covered the aspect of file and module organization. How should code be grouped into files and modules?

To answer this question, we recommend something called **the workshop model**. Imagine a physical workshop with pegboards, shelves, jars, toolboxes, and larger equipment on the floor. When speaking about code architecture, experts often talk about different organizational strategies. It is possible to group code by type, by purpose, by project layer, or by convenience. There are infinite possible strategies, and these are just four common ones. None of these are wrong, though we recommend against choosing any one specifically. Our reason is simple—choose all of them. Nuts and bolts can be organized into jars (by type). Hand tools can be placed in a toolbox (by purpose). Large tools can be placed on the floor (by project layer). Common tools can be hung on a pegboard (by convenience). None of these strategies are invalid, and all of them can be used in the same workshop (project).

In this chapter, we will reorganize the project as it grows. We will combine the principles of planning and architecture that we previously introduced with new concepts of code organization to develop a large software project that is navigable and maintainable.

The learning outcomes of this chapter are as follows:

- Recognizing and applying by type organization
- Recognizing and applying by purpose organization
- Recognizing and applying by layer organization
- Recognizing and applying by convenience organization
- Minimizing code waste during project reorganization

Technical requirements

A recent version of Rust is necessary to run the examples provided:

https://www.rust-lang.org/en-US/install.html

This chapter's code is also available on GitHub:

https://github.com/PacktPublishing/Hands-On-Functional-Programming-in-RUST

Specific installation and build instructions are also included in each chapter's README.md file.

Shipping a product without sacrificing quality

The client has finished negotiating with your sales team—you won the contract. Now that the contract is signed, your team is on task to bring the simulation up to specification to run all of the elevator systems. The client has provided specifications for each of the three buildings, elevators, motor control, and braking systems. You also learn that the elevator motors have intelligent motor control software that regulates internal voltage and current dynamically. To control the motor, you will only be expected to supply the desired force output. The full specifications are as follows:

- For building 1, there are the following:
  - **Floor heights**: 8m, 4m, 4m, 4m, 4m
  - **Elevator weight**: 1,200 kg

- **Elevator motor**: Maximum 50,000 N
- **Elevator driver**: Software interface supplied
- For building 2, there are the following:
    - **Floor heights**: 5m, 5m, 5m, 5m, 5m, 5m, 5m, 5m
    - **Elevator weight**: 1,350 kg
    - **Elevator motor**: maximum 1,00,000 N
    - **Elevator driver**: Software interface supplied
- For building 3, there are the following:
    - **Floor heights**: 6m, 4m, 4m, 4m
    - **Elevator weight**: 1,400 kg
    - **Elevator motor**: Maximum 90,000 N
    - **Elevator driver**: Software interface supplied

The program now needs to work in operational mode, where new floor requests are accepted and added to the queue. The simulation should also continue to work, now with all three building specifications. The simulation should verify that promised performance and quality metrics are all satisfied. Other than that, your team is free to develop the project as you see fit.

You decide that now is a good time to rethink the organization of the project, with significant new changes required. Using good architecture and project organization practices, you will move code around accordingly to group components orderly and conveniently.

Reorganizing the project

Now that we have some ideas of good project architecture, let's plan the project's reorganization. Let's list the possible workshop organization methods:

- By type
- By purpose
- By layer
- By convenience

The by type organization should be used for workshop nuts and bolts type components. Nuts and bolts are highly uniform components that have a different diameter, length, grade, and so on. We have a few good matches here, so let's list objects and interfaces that could be grouped this way:

- Motors
- Buildings
- Elevator controllers/drivers

The by purpose organization should be used for miscellaneous tools that have a common purpose. We have some good candidates for this style of organization, too:

- Transport planning (static/dynamic)
- The physical interface to an elevator

The by layer organization should be used for distinct architectural components that fit well within normal program logic. An example of this would be our physics layer, which is logically independent of other modules. The physics layer exists solely to store constants, formulas, and modeling procedures. Here, we group this by layer:

- Physics modeling

The by convenience organization should be used for common or difficult components. Executables are a good fit for this type of organization because they are always an endpoint, not a library, and don't typically fit into any other organization well:

- Simulation executable
- Analyze executable
- Physical elevator driver executable

Planning content of files by type

These files will be organized using the by type method.

Organizing the motor_controllers.rs module

All motors will be grouped by type in the `motor_controller.rs` module. There will be three motors with varying properties. This module should provide a trait interface to all motors as well as each implementation. The trait should define a method to generate a motor input from the desired force output and also a method to accept a motor input to generate a force. The module must also link in the binary drivers for each motor controller. The old motor controller logic to dynamically control the elevator motor will be moved into a new file called `motion_controllers.rs`. The following should be defined in this module:

- Motor input trait
- Motor controller trait
- Motor input 1 implementation
- Motor controller 1 implementation
- Motor input 2 implementation
- Motor controller 2 implementation
- Motor input 3 implementation
- Motor controller 3 implementation

Organizing the buildings.rs module

All building specifications will be grouped by type in the `building.rs` module. There will be three building specifications. The building should encapsulate all aspects of elevator behavior and control, as well as a specification for the building itself. The module should contain the following:

- Building trait
- Building 1 implementation
- Building 2 implementation
- Building 3 implementation

Planning content of files by purpose

These files will be organized using the by purpose method.

Organizing the motion_controllers.rs module

Motion controllers will be organized by purpose. The motion controllers will be responsible for tracking elevator state to control the motor's dynamics. The motion controllers module should contain the following:

- Motion Controller trait
- Smooth Motion Controller implementation

Organizing the trip_planning.rs module

Trip planning will be organized by purpose. The planner should work in two modes: static and dynamic. For static mode, the planner should accept a list of floor requests to process. For dynamic mode, the planner should accept floor requests as they come dynamically and add them to the queue. The planner module should contain the following:

- Planner trait
- Static planner implementation
- Dynamic planner implementation

Organizing the elevator_drivers.rs module

All elevator drivers will be organized by purpose in the `elevator_driver.rs` module. There are three elevator drivers that provide binary interfaces to be linked. The `elevator driver` module should contain a trait to define an interface to elevator drivers as well as the three implementations. The `planner` module should contain the following:

- Elevator driver trait
- Elevator driver 1 implementation
- Elevator driver 2 implementation
- Elevator driver 3 implementation

Planning content of files by layer

These files will be organized using the by layer method.

Organizing the physics.rs module

The `physics` module will group all physics-related code by layer. There will be miscellaneous code here, though it should all fit in the form of some sort of simulation or prediction. The module should contain the following:

- Unit conversions
- Formula implementations
- Any other logic required for the simulation or operation of elevators
- Physics simulation loop

Organizing the data_recorder.rs module

The data recorder module will move the `DataRecorder` trait and implementation into its own module. It should contain the following:

- The `DataRecorder` trait
- Simple data recorder implementation

Planning the content of files by convenience

These files will be organized using the by convenience method.

Organizing the simulate_trip.rs executable

The `simulate_trip.rs` executable will be organized by convenience. The scope of the trip simulation executable has not changed significantly. This file should contain the following:

- Argument and input parsing
- Data logger definition
- Simulation setup
- Run simulation

Organizing the analyze_trip.rs executable

The `analyze_trip.rs` executable will be organized by convenience. The scope of the analyze trip executable has not changed significantly. This file should contain the following:

- Argument and input parsing
- Check specifications for acceptance or rejection

Organizing the operate_elevator.rs executable

The `operate_elevator.rs` executable will be organized by convenience. The operate elevator executable should closely resemble the simulate elevator executable logic. This file should contain the following:

- Argument and input parsing
- Setup elevator drivers to match specified building code
- Run the elevator with dynamic planning

Mapping code changes and additions

Now that we have organized our concepts, data structures, and logic into files, we can now proceed with the normal process to transform requirements into code. For each module, we will look at the required elements and produce code to satisfy those requirements.

Here, we break down all code development steps by module. Different modules have different organizations, so pay attention for patterns regarding organization and code development.

Developing code by type

These files will be organized using the by type method.

Writing the motor_controllers.rs module

The new `motor_controller` module serves as an adapter to all of the linked motor drivers and their interfaces, and provides a single uniform interface. Let's see how:

1. First, let's link all the drivers from the software provided into our program:

```
use libc::c_int;

#[link(name = "motor1")]
extern {
    pub fn motor1_adjust_motor(target_force: c_int) -> c_int;
}

#[link(name = "motor2")]
extern {
    pub fn motor2_adjust_motor(target_force: c_int) -> c_int;
}

#[link(name = "motor3")]
extern {
    pub fn motor3_adjust_motor(target_force: c_int) -> c_int;
}
```

This section tells our program to link to statically compiled libraries named something like `libmotor1.a`, `libmotor2.a`, and `libmotor3.a`. Our example chapter also contains the source and build script for these libraries, so you can inspect each one. In a full project, there are many ways to link to an external binary library, this being only one of many options.

2. Next, we should make a trait for `MotorInput` and a generic `MotorDriver` interface, including implementations for each motor. The code is as follows:

```
#[derive(Clone,Serialize,Deserialize,Debug)]
pub enum MotorInput
{
    Motor1 { target_force: f64 },
    Motor2 { target_force: f64 },
    Motor3 { target_force: f64 },
}

pub trait MotorDriver
{
    fn adjust_motor(&self, input: MotorInput);
}

struct Motor1;
impl MotorDriver for Motor1 { ... }

//Motor 2

//Motor 3
```

3. Next, we should implement the motor controller trait and implementations. The motor controller should wrap motor information and drivers into a uniform interface. The `MotorDriver` and `MotorController` trait here are coerced into a simple upward/downward force model. Therefore, the relation between driver and controller is one-to-one and cannot be completely abstracted into a common trait. The code for it is as follows:

```
pub trait MotorController
{
    fn adjust_motor(&self, f: f64);
    fn max_force(&self) -> f64;
}

pub struct MotorController1
{
    motor: Motor1
}

impl MotorController for MotorController1 { ... }

//Motor Controller 2 ...

//Motor Controller 3 ...
```

The entire code for these is present in the GitHub repository at: `https://github.com/PacktPublishing/Hands-On-Functional-Programming-in-RUST`.

Writing the buildings.rs module

The building module is again grouped by type. There should be a common trait interface that is implemented by the three buildings. The building traits and structures should additionally wrap and expose interfaces to appropriate elevator drivers and motor controllers. The code is as follows:

1. First, we define the `Building` trait:

```
pub trait Building
{
    fn get_elevator_driver(&self) -> Box<ElevatorDriver>;
    fn get_motor_controller(&self) -> Box<MotorController>;
    fn get_floor_heights(&self) -> Vec<f64>;
    fn get_carriage_weight(&self) -> f64;
    fn clone(&self) -> Box<Building>;
    fn serialize(&self) -> u64;
}
```

2. Then, we define a `deserialize` helper function:

```
pub fn deserialize(n: u64) -> Box<Building>
{
    if n==1 {
        Box::new(Building1)
    } else if n==2 {
        Box::new(Building2)
    } else {
        Box::new(Building3)
    }
}
```

3. Then, we define some miscellaneous helper functions:

```
pub fn getCarriageFloor(floorHeights: Vec<f64>, height: f64) -> u64
{
    let mut c = 0.0;
    for (fi, fht) in floorHeights.iter().enumerate() {
        c += fht;
        if height <= c {
            return (fi as u64)
        }
    }
    (floorHeights.len()-1) as u64
}

pub fn getCumulativeFloorHeight(heights: Vec<f64>, floor: u64) -> f64
{
    heights.iter().take(floor as usize).sum()
}
```

4. Finally, we define the buildings and their trait implementations:

```
pub struct Building1;
impl Building for Building1 { ... }

//Building 2

//Building 3
```

Developing code by purpose

These files will be organized using the by purpose method.

Writing the motion_controllers.rs module

The old logic from `motor_controllers.rs` for dynamically adjusting motor force will be moved to this module. The `SmoothMotionController` does not change much and the code becomes as follows:

```
pub trait MotionController
{
    fn init(&mut self, esp: Box<Building>, est: ElevatorState);
    fn adjust(&mut self, est: &ElevatorState, dst: u64) -> f64;
}

pub struct SmoothMotionController
{
    pub esp: Box<Building>,
    pub timestamp: f64
}

impl MotionController for SmoothMotionController
{
    ...
}
```

Writing the trip_planning.rs module

The trip planner should work in static and dynamic modes. The basic structure is a FIFO queue, pushing requests into the queue, and popping the oldest element. We may be able to unify both static and dynamic modes into a single implementation, which would look like the following.

Trip planning will be organized by purpose. The planner should work in two modes—static and dynamic. For static mode, the planner should accept a list of floor requests to process. For dynamic mode, the planner should accept floor requests as they come dynamically and add them to the queue. The planner module should contain the following:

```
use std::collections::VecDeque;

pub struct FloorRequests
{
    pub requests: VecDeque<u64>
}

pub trait RequestQueue
{
```

```
    fn add_request(&mut self, req: u64);
    fn add_requests(&mut self, reqs: &Vec<u64>);
    fn pop_request(&mut self) -> Option<u64>;
}

impl RequestQueue for FloorRequests
{
    fn add_request(&mut self, req: u64)
    {
        self.requests.push_back(req);
    }
    fn add_requests(&mut self, reqs: &Vec<u64>)
    {
        for req in reqs
        {
            self.requests.push_back(*req);
        }
    }
    fn pop_request(&mut self) -> Option<u64>
    {
        self.requests.pop_front()
    }
}
```

Writing the elevator_drivers.rs module

The elevator drivers module should interface with the static libraries provided and
additionally provide a common interface to all elevator drivers. The code looks like the
following:

```
use libc::c_int;

#[link(name = "elevator1")]
extern {
    pub fn elevator1_poll_floor_request() -> c_int;
}

#[link(name = "elevator2")]
extern {
    pub fn elevator2_poll_floor_request() -> c_int;
}

#[link(name = "elevator3")]
extern {
    pub fn elevator3_poll_floor_request() -> c_int;
}
```

```
pub trait ElevatorDriver
{
    fn poll_floor_request(&self) -> Option<u64>;
}

pub struct ElevatorDriver1;
impl ElevatorDriver for ElevatorDriver1
{
    fn poll_floor_request(&self) -> Option<u64>
    {
        unsafe {
            let req = elevator1_poll_floor_request();
            if req > 0 {
                Some(req as u64)
            } else {
                None
            }
        }
    }
}

//Elevator Driver 2

//Elevator Driver 3
```

Developing code by layer

These files will be organized using the by layer method.

Writing the physics.rs module

The physics module has become much smaller. It now contains a few struct definitions and constants and the central `simulate_elevator` method. The result is as follows:

```
#[derive(Clone,Debug,Serialize,Deserialize)]
pub struct ElevatorState {
    pub timestamp: f64,
    pub location: f64,
    pub velocity: f64,
    pub acceleration: f64,
    pub motor_input: f64
}

pub const MAX_JERK: f64 = 0.2;
```

```
pub const MAX_ACCELERATION: f64 = 2.0;
pub const MAX_VELOCITY: f64 = 5.0;

pub fn simulate_elevator(esp: Box<Building>, est: ElevatorState,
floor_requests: &mut Box<RequestQueue>,
                         mc: &mut Box<MotionController>, dr: &mut
Box<DataRecorder>)
{
    //immutable input becomes mutable local state
    let mut esp = esp.clone();
    let mut est = est.clone();

    //initialize MotorController and DataController
    mc.init(esp.clone(), est.clone());
    dr.init(esp.clone(), est.clone());

    //5. Loop while there are remaining floor requests
    let original_ts = Instant::now();
    thread::sleep(time::Duration::from_millis(1));
    let mut next_floor = floor_requests.pop_request();
    while let Some(dst) = next_floor
    {
        //5.1. Update location, velocity, and acceleration
        let now = Instant::now();
        let ts = now.duration_since(original_ts)
                   .as_fractional_secs();
        let dt = ts - est.timestamp;
        est.timestamp = ts;

        est.location = est.location + est.velocity * dt;
        est.velocity = est.velocity + est.acceleration * dt;
        est.acceleration = {
            let F = est.motor_input;
            let m = esp.get_carriage_weight();
            -9.8 + F/m
        };

        //5.2. If next floor request in queue is satisfied, then remove
from queue
        if (est.location -
getCumulativeFloorHeight(esp.get_floor_heights(), dst)).abs() < 0.01 &&
            est.velocity.abs() < 0.01
        {
            est.velocity = 0.0;
            next_floor = floor_requests.pop_request();
        }

        //5.4. Print realtime statistics
```

```
        dr.poll(est.clone(), dst);

        //5.3. Adjust motor control to process next floor request
        est.motor_input = mc.poll(est.clone(), dst);

        thread::sleep(time::Duration::from_millis(1));
    }
}
```

Writing the data_recorders.rs module

To separate responsibilities and not let individual modules get too big, we should move the data recorder implementation out of the simulation and into its own module. The result is as follows:

1. Define the DataRecorder trait:

```
pub trait DataRecorder
{
    fn init(&mut self, esp: Box<Building>, est: ElevatorState);
    fn record(&mut self, est: ElevatorState, dst: u64);
    fn summary(&mut self);
}
```

2. Define the SimpleDataRecorder struct:

```
struct SimpleDataRecorder<W: Write>
{
    esp: Box<Building>,
    termwidth: u64,
    termheight: u64,
    stdout: raw::RawTerminal<W>,
    log: File,
    record_location: Vec<f64>,
    record_velocity: Vec<f64>,
    record_acceleration: Vec<f64>,
    record_force: Vec<f64>,
}
```

3. Define the SimpleDataRecorder constructor:

```
pub fn newSimpleDataRecorder(esp: Box<Building>) -> Box<DataRecorder>
{
    let termsize = termion::terminal_size().ok();
    Box::new(SimpleDataRecorder {
        esp: esp.clone(),
```

```
        termwidth: termsize.map(|(w,_)| w-2).expect("termwidth") as u64,
        termheight: termsize.map(|(_,h)| h-2).expect("termheight") as
u64,
        stdout: io::stdout().into_raw_mode().unwrap(),
        log: File::create("simulation.log").expect("log file"),
        record_location: Vec::new(),
        record_velocity: Vec::new(),
        record_acceleration: Vec::new(),
        record_force: Vec::new()
    })
}
```

4. Define the `SimpleDataRecorder` implementation of the `DataRecorder` trait:

```
impl<W: Write> DataRecorder for SimpleDataRecorder<W>
{
    fn init(&mut self, esp: Box<Building>, est: ElevatorState)
    {
        ...
    }
    fn record(&mut self, est: ElevatorState, dst: u64)
        ...
    }
    fn summary(&mut self)
    {
        ...
    }
}
```

5. Define the miscellaneous helper functions:

```
fn variable_summary<W: Write>(stdout: &mut raw::RawTerminal<W>, vname:
String, data: &Vec<f64>) {
    let (avg, dev) = variable_summary_stats(data);
    variable_summary_print(stdout, vname, avg, dev);
}

fn variable_summary_stats(data: &Vec<f64>) -> (f64, f64)
{
    //calculate statistics
    let N = data.len();
    let sum = data.iter().sum::<f64>();
    let avg = sum / (N as f64);
    let dev = (
        data.clone().into_iter()
        .map(|v| (v - avg).powi(2))
        .sum::<f64>()
        / (N as f64)
```

```
    ).sqrt();
    (avg, dev)
}

fn variable_summary_print<W: Write>(stdout: &mut raw::RawTerminal<W>,
vname: String, avg: f64, dev: f64)
{
    //print formatted output
    writeln!(stdout, "Average of {:25}{:.6}", vname, avg);
    writeln!(stdout, "Standard deviation of {:14}{:.6}", vname, dev);
    writeln!(stdout, "");
}
```

Developing code by convenience

These files will be organized using the by convenience method.

Writing the simulate_trip.rs executable

The simulate trip changes quite a bit because the DataRecorder logic has been removed. The initialization of the simulation is also very different from before. The end result is as follows:

1. Initialize ElevatorState:

```
//1. Store location, velocity, and acceleration state
//2. Store motor input target force
let mut est = ElevatorState {
    timestamp: 0.0,
    location: 0.0,
    velocity: 0.0,
    acceleration: 0.0,
    motor_input: 0.0
};
```

2. Initialize the building description and floor requests:

```
//3. Store input building description and floor requests
let mut esp: Box<Building> = Box::new(Building1);
let mut floor_requests: Box<RequestQueue> = Box::new(FloorRequests {
    requests: Vec::new()
});
```

3. Parse the input and store it as building description and floor requests:

```
//4. Parse input and store as building description and floor requests
match env::args().nth(1) {
    Some(ref fp) if *fp == "-".to_string()  => {
        ...
    },
    None => {
        ...
    },
    Some(fp)  => {
        ...
    }
}
```

4. Initialize the data recorder and motion controller:

```
let mut dr: Box<DataRecorder> = newSimpleDataRecorder(esp.clone());
let mut mc: Box<MotionController> = Box::new(SmoothMotionController {
    timestamp: 0.0,
    esp: esp.clone()
});
```

5. Run the elevator simulation:

```
simulate_elevator(esp, est, &mut floor_requests, &mut mc, &mut dr);
```

6. Print the simulation summary:

```
dr.summary();
```

Writing the analyze_trip.rs executable

The analyze trip executable will only change a little bit, but only to accommodate symbols that have been moved and types that are now serializable with SerDe. The result is as follows:

1. Define the Trip data structure:

```
#[derive(Clone)]
struct Trip {
    dst: u64,
    up: f64,
    down: f64
}
```

2. Initialize the variables:

```
let simlog = File::open("simulation.log").expect("read simulation
log");
let mut simlog = BufReader::new(&simlog);
let mut jerk = 0.0;
let mut prev_est: Option<ElevatorState> = None;
let mut dst_timing: Vec<Trip> = Vec::new();
let mut start_location = 0.0;
```

3. Iterate over log lines and initialize the elevator specification:

```
let mut first_line = String::new();
let len = simlog.read_line(&mut first_line).unwrap();
let spec: u64 = serde_json::from_str(&first_line).unwrap();
let esp: Box<Building> = buildings::deserialize(spec);

for line in simlog.lines() {
    let l = line.unwrap();
    //Check elevator state records
}
```

4. Check the elevator state records:

```
let (est, dst): (ElevatorState,u64) =
serde_json::from_str(&l).unwrap();
let dl = dst_timing.len();
if dst_timing.len()==0 || dst_timing[dl-1].dst != dst {
    dst_timing.push(Trip { dst:dst, up:0.0, down:0.0 });
}

if let Some(prev_est) = prev_est {
    let dt = est.timestamp - prev_est.timestamp;
    if est.velocity > 0.0 {
        dst_timing[dl-1].up += dt;
    } else {
        dst_timing[dl-1].down += dt;
    }
    let da = (est.acceleration - prev_est.acceleration).abs();
    jerk = (jerk * (1.0 - dt)) + (da * dt);
    if jerk.abs() > 0.22 {
        panic!("jerk is outside of acceptable limits: {} {:?}", jerk,
est)
    }
} else {
    start_location = est.location;
}
```

```
if est.acceleration.abs() > 2.2 {
    panic!("acceleration is outside of acceptable limits: {:?}", est)
}

if est.velocity.abs() > 5.5 {
    panic!("velocity is outside of acceptable limits: {:?}", est)
}

prev_est = Some(est);
```

5. Check that the elevator does not backup:

```
//elevator should not backup
let mut total_time = 0.0;
let mut total_direct = 0.0;
for trip in dst_timing.clone()
{
    total_time += (trip.up + trip.down);
    if trip.up > trip.down {
        total_direct += trip.up;
    } else {
        total_direct += trip.down;
    }
}

if (total_direct / total_time) < 0.9 {
    panic!("elevator back up is too common: {}", total_direct /
total_time)
}
```

6. Check that the trips finish within 20% of their theoretical limit:

```
let mut trip_start_location = start_location;
let mut theoretical_time = 0.0;
let floor_heights = esp.get_floor_heights();
for trip in dst_timing.clone()
{
    let next_floor = getCumulativeFloorHeight(floor_heights.clone(),
trip.dst);
    let d = (trip_start_location - next_floor).abs();
    theoretical_time += (
        2.0*(MAX_ACCELERATION / MAX_JERK) +
        2.0*(MAX_JERK / MAX_ACCELERATION) +
        d / MAX_VELOCITY
    );
    trip_start_location = next_floor;
}
```

```
if total_time > (theoretical_time * 1.2) {
    panic!("elevator moves to slow {} {}", total_time, theoretical_time
* 1.2)
}
```

Writing the operate_elevator.rs executable

The operate elevator is very similar to the `simulate_trip.rs` and physics `run_simulation` code. The most significant difference is the ability to continue running while dynamically accepting new requests and adjusting motor control using the linked libraries. In the main executable, we follow the same logical process as before, adjusted for new names and type signatures:

1. Initialize `ElevatorState`:

```
//1. Store location, velocity, and acceleration state
//2. Store motor input target force
let mut est = ElevatorState {
    timestamp: 0.0,
    location: 0.0,
    velocity: 0.0,
    acceleration: 0.0,
    motor_input: 0.0
};
```

2. Initialize `MotionController`:

```
let mut mc: Box<MotionController> = Box::new(SmoothMotionController {
    timestamp: 0.0,
    esp: esp.clone()
});
mc.init(esp.clone(), est.clone());
```

3. Start the operating loop to process incoming floor requests:

```
//5. Loop continuously checking for new floor requests
let original_ts = Instant::now();
thread::sleep(time::Duration::from_millis(1));
let mut next_floor = floor_requests.pop_request();
while true
{
    if let Some(dst) = next_floor {
        //process floor request
    }
```

```
//check for dynamic floor requests
if let Some(dst) = esp.get_elevator_driver().poll_floor_request()
{
    floor_requests.add_request(dst);
}
}
```

4. In the processing loop, update the physics approximations:

```
//5.1. Update location, velocity, and acceleration
let now = Instant::now();
let ts = now.duration_since(original_ts)
            .as_fractional_secs();
let dt = ts - est.timestamp;
est.timestamp = ts;

est.location = est.location + est.velocity * dt;
est.velocity = est.velocity + est.acceleration * dt;
est.acceleration = {
    let F = est.motor_input;
    let m = esp.get_carriage_weight();
    -9.8 + F/m
};
```

5. If the current floor request is satisfied, remove it from the queue:

```
//5.2. If next floor request in queue is satisfied, then remove from
queue
if (est.location - getCumulativeFloorHeight(esp.get_floor_heights(),
dst)).abs() < 0.01 && est.velocity.abs() < 0.01
{
    est.velocity = 0.0;
    next_floor = floor_requests.pop_request();
}
```

6. Adjust the motor control:

```
//5.3. Adjust motor control to process next floor request
est.motor_input = mc.poll(est.clone(), dst);

//Adjust motor
esp.get_motor_controller().adjust_motor(est.motor_input);
```

Reflecting on the project structure

Now that we have developed code to organize and connect different elevator functions, as well as three executables to simulate, analyze, and operate the elevators, let's ask ourselves this—how does it all fit together, and have we done a good job architecting this project thus far?

Reviewing this chapter, we can quickly see that we have made use of four different code organization techniques. At a more casual level, the code seems to fall into categories, as follows:

- **Luggage**: Like drivers that need to be connected, but may be difficult to work with
- **Nuts**, **bolts**, and **gears**: Like structs and traits, we have a lot of control of how to design
- **Deliverables**: Like executables, these must fulfill a specific requirement

We have organized all deliverables by convenience; all luggage by type or by purpose; and nuts, bolts, and gears have been organized by type, by purpose, or by layer. The result could be worse, and organizing by a different standard does not imply that the code will change significantly. Overall, the deliverables are supported by fairly maintainable code and the project is going in a good direction.

Summary

In this chapter, we examined four code organization principles that can be used alone or in combination to develop well-structured projects. The four principles of organization by type, by purpose, by layer, and by convenience are helpful perspectives for inspiring good architecture choices when structuring larger projects. The larger and more complex a project becomes, the more important these decisions become, though simultaneously more difficult to change.

Applying these concepts, we restructured the entire project using each principle to a varying degree. We also incorporated significant changes to allow interfacing with external libraries and applied operations of the elevator, as opposed to a closed simulation. Now, the elevators of three buildings should be capable of running entirely on the software developed here.

In the next chapter, we will learn about mutability and ownership. We have covered these concepts to a certain degree already, but the next chapter will demand a much more in-depth understanding of specific details and limitations.

Questions

1. What are four ways of grouping code into modules?
2. What does FFI stand for?
3. Why are unsafe blocks necessary?
4. Is it ever safe to use unsafe blocks?
5. What is the difference between a `libc::c_int` and an `int32`?
6. Can linked libraries define functions with the same name?
7. What type of files can be linked into a Rust project?

6
Mutability, Ownership, and Pure Functions

Rust has introduced some new concepts of its own with respect to object ownership. These safeguards protect the developer from certain classes of errors, such as double free memory or hanging pointers, but also create constraints that can feel unmerited at times. Functional programming may help ease some of this conflict by encouraging the use of immutable data and pure functions.

In this chapter, we will look at a case of ownership gone wrong. You will inherit code that has been abandoned as being too difficult to work with. Your job in this chapter will be to address the problems that the previous team were unable to overcome. To achieve this, you will need to use much of what you have learned so far, along with a gained understanding of the specific behaviors and constraints of ownership in Rust.

Learning outcomes:

- Recognizing anti-patterns of complex ownership
- Learning specific rules of complex ownership
- Using immutable data to prevent anti-patterns of ownership
- Using pure functions to prevent anti-patterns of ownership

Technical requirements

A recent version of Rust is necessary to run the examples provided:

```
https://www.rust-lang.org/en-US/install.html
```

This chapter's code is also available on GitHub:

`https://github.com/PacktPublishing/Hands-On-Functional-Programming-in-RUST`

Specific installation and build instructions are also included in each chapter's `README.md` file.

Recognizing anti-patterns of ownership

Consider the following situation.

Congratulations, you have inherited legacy code. A previous team responsible for developing privileged access modules for elevators has been moved to a different project. They successfully developed code libraries to interface with a range of microcontrollers. However, while developing the access logic in Rust, they found object ownership to be very complicated and were unable to develop software that was compatible with Rust.

Your task in this chapter will be to analyze their code, look for possible solutions, then create a library to support privileged access for your elevators. To clarify, privileged access refers to override codes and keys made available to emergency services such as police, firemen, and so on.

Inspecting the microcontroller drivers

The microcontroller drivers are written in other languages and exposed to Rust through the **foreign function interface** (FFI) feature. An FFI is a way of connecting Rust code to libraries written in other languages. The following are the symbols defined in the foreign library and bindings in `src/magic.rs`.

This function issues an override code to the library and subsystem, as follows:

```
fn issue_override_code(code: c_int)
```

When an override code is entered, it will be exposed through this function. The higher layers should interpret what the override codes mean to potentially enter emergency operation modes or other maintenance functions, as follows:

```
fn poll_override_code() -> c_int
```

When an override mode has been established and the emergency service worker enters a floor, this method will be called. Floor requests from emergency modes should take precedence over normal `elevator` operation:

```
fn poll_override_input_floor()
```

Error codes occurring from the `override` operation will be exposed through this function. Issues such as invalid override codes will be presented for higher layers to decide how to respond:

```
fn poll_override_error() -> c_int
```

If an override code is entered, an authorized override session will be created:

```
fn poll_override_session() -> *const c_void
```

After an override session is complete, it should be freed to release resources and reset state:

```
fn free_override_session(session: *const c_void)
```

If a physical key access is initiated to an elevator, then this method will expose the result:

```
fn poll_physical_override_privileged_session() -> *const c_void
```

If a physical key access is initiated by an administrator, then this method will expose the result, as follows:

```
fn poll_physical_override_admin_session() -> *const c_void
```

This function will force the elevator into manual operation mode:

```
fn override_manual_mode()
```

This function will force the elevator into normal operation mode:

```
fn override_normal_mode()
```

This function will reset the elevator state:

```
fn override_reset_state()
```

This function will perform a timed flashing pattern of lights on the elevator control panel:

```
fn elevator_display_flash(pattern: c_int)
```

This function will toggle the light for a button or other symbol on the elevator control panel:

```
fn elevator_display_toggle_light(light_id: c_int)
```

This function will alter the display color of a light on the elevator control panel:

```
fn elevator_display_set_light_color(light_id: c_int, color: int)
```

Inspecting the type and trait definitions

The Rust type and trait definitions left behind were primarily intended to wrap the library interfaces. Let's look quickly through the symbols defined in src/admin.rs to familiarize ourselves with how the library was intended to work.

Defining the OverrideCode enum

The OverrideCode enum gives typesafe definitions and names to the different override codes from the linked library. This code associates named enum values with the numerical enumerated values returned or sent to the FFI. Notice the syntax pattern assigning integer values to each enum element:

```
pub enum OverrideCode {
    IssueOverride = 1,
    IssuePrivileged = 2,
    IssueAdmin = 3,
    IssueInputFloor = 4,
    IssueManualMode = 5,
    IssueNormalMode = 6,
    IssueFlash = 7,
    IssueToggleLight = 8,
    IssueSetLightColor = 9,
}

pub fn toOverrideCode(i: i32) -> OverrideCode {
    match i {
        1 => OverrideCode::IssueOverride,
        2 => OverrideCode::IssuePrivileged,
        3 => OverrideCode::IssueAdmin,
        4 => OverrideCode::IssueInputFloor,
        5 => OverrideCode::IssueManualMode,
        6 => OverrideCode::IssueNormalMode,
        7 => OverrideCode::IssueFlash,
        8 => OverrideCode::IssueToggleLight,
```

```
        9 => OverrideCode::IssueSetLightColor,
        _ => panic!("Unexpected override code: {}", i)
    }
}
```

Defining the ErrorCode enum

Similar to `OverrideCode`, the `ErrorCode` enum defines typesafe labels for each of the library error codes. There is also a helper function to cast integers into the enum type:

```
pub enum ErrorCode {
    DoubleAuthorize = 1,
    DoubleFree = 2,
    AccessDenied = 3,
}

pub fn toErrorCode(i: i32) -> ErrorCode {
    match i {
        1 => ErrorCode::DoubleAuthorize,
        2 => ErrorCode::DoubleFree,
        3 => ErrorCode::AccessDenied,
        _ => panic!("Unexpected error code: {}", i)
    }
}
```

Defining the AuthorizedSession struct and deconstructor

The `AuthorizedSession` struct wraps a session pointer from the library. This struct also implements the `Drop` trait, which is called when the object goes out of scope. The `free_override_session` call here is very important and should be noted as a potential source of problems:

```
#[derive(Clone)]
pub struct AuthorizedSession
{
    session: *const c_void
}

impl Drop for AuthorizedSession {
    fn drop(&mut self) {
        unsafe {
            magic::free_override_session(self.session);
        }
```

```
    }
  }
```

Authorizing sessions

To authorize a session, there are three steps:

1. Authorize the session
2. Poll and retrieve the session object
3. Check for errors

The results of these functions are `Result` objects, which will be a common pattern in this library:

```
pub fn authorize_override() -> Result<AuthorizedSession,ErrorCode>
{
  let session = unsafe {
    magic::issue_override_code(OverrideCode::IssueOverride as i32);
    magic::poll_override_session()
  };
  let session = AuthorizedSession {
    session: session
  };
  check_error(session)
}

pub fn authorize_privileged() -> Result<AuthorizedSession,ErrorCode>
{ ... }

pub fn authorize_admin() -> Result<AuthorizedSession,ErrorCode>
{ ... }
```

Checking errors and resetting state

There are two simple utility functions available that reset state and check for errors. The code wraps the FFI functions in unsafe blocks and converts errors into `Result` values. The code is as follows:

```
pub fn reset_state()
{
  unsafe {
    magic::override_reset_state();
  }
}
```

```
pub fn check_error<T>(t: T) -> Result<T,ErrorCode>
{
    let err = unsafe {
        magic::poll_override_error()
    };
    if err==0 {
        Result::Ok(t)
    } else {
        Result::Err(toErrorCode(err))
    }
}
```

Privileged commands

Privileged commands must be authorized before being called, otherwise the command will be denied. Errors are checked after each operation and a `Result` value is returned:

```
pub fn input_floor(floor: i32) -> Result<(),ErrorCode>
{
    unsafe {
        magic::override_input_floor(floor);
    }
    check_error(())
}

pub fn manual_mode() -> Result<(),ErrorCode>
{
    unsafe {
        magic::override_manual_mode();
    }
    check_error(())
}

pub fn normal_mode() -> Result<(),ErrorCode>
{
    unsafe {
        magic::override_normal_mode();
    }
    check_error(())
}
```

Normal commands

Normal commands do not require an authorized session to be called. Errors are checked after each call and a `Result` value is returned:

```
pub fn flash(pattern: i32) -> Result<(),ErrorCode>
{
   unsafe {
      magic::elevator_display_flash(pattern);
   }
   check_error(())
}

pub fn toggle_light(light_id: i32) -> Result<(),ErrorCode>
{
   unsafe {
      magic::elevator_display_toggle_light(light_id);
   }
   check_error(())
}

pub fn set_light_color(light_id: i32, color: i32) -> Result<(),ErrorCode>
{
   unsafe {
      magic::elevator_display_set_light_color(light_id, color);
   }
   check_error(())
}
```

Querying library and session state

Several functions that query the library and session state are available, mostly for debugging purposes:

```
pub fn is_override() -> bool
{
   unsafe {
      magic::is_override() != 0
   }
}

pub fn is_privileged() -> bool
{
   unsafe {
      magic::is_privileged() != 0
   }
```

```
    }

pub fn is_admin() -> bool
{
    unsafe {
        magic::is_admin() != 0
    }
}
```

Inspecting the foreign library tests

The previous team seemed very confident in the library subsystem that they developed; however, they found Rust code difficult to work with. The tests make this problem apparent. Two test sets seem to support the notion that the library works as intended, but the Rust components fail in edge cases. It will be your responsibility to pick up the pieces and salvage the project.

Looking at the library tests in `src/tests/magic.rs`, the intended behavior is as follows:

- Override codes are issued to the subsystem through either elevator control panel or from the software directly
- Status information and authorization sessions are accessed through the `poll` functions
- Authorization sessions must be freed before others can authorize
- In override mode, privileged commands may be issued, such as:
  - Change elevator to manual operation
  - Use elevator display panel to communicate
- Privileged commands may not be issued without an active session

All library tests are passing, confirming the correct behavior of the library under the limited conditions tested. It should also be noted that the library is a bit obtuse in how it handles state, events, and sessions. These patterns are common in linked libraries, but to see the pattern, let's look at the resulting code in Rust.

Issuing override codes

This set of tests for the FFI functions confirms that issued command codes are received by the library:

```
#[test]
fn issue_override_code() {
    unsafe {
        magic::override_reset_state();
        magic::issue_override_code(1);
        assert!(magic::poll_override_code() == 1);
        assert!(magic::poll_override_error() == 0);
    }
}

#[test]
fn issue_privileged_code() {
    unsafe {
        magic::override_reset_state();
        magic::issue_override_code(2);
        assert!(magic::poll_override_code() == 2);
        assert!(magic::poll_override_error() == 0);
    }
}

#[test]
fn issue_admin_code() {
    unsafe {
        magic::override_reset_state();
        magic::issue_override_code(3);
        assert!(magic::poll_override_code() == 3);
        assert!(magic::poll_override_error() == 0);
    }
}
```

Accessing status information and sessions

These tests confirm that authorizing sessions and releasing sessions works correctly:

```
#[test]
fn authorize_override_success() {
    unsafe {
        magic::override_reset_state();
        magic::issue_override_code(1);
        let session = magic::poll_override_session();
        assert!(session != (0 as *const c_void));
```

```
            magic::free_override_session(session);
            assert!(magic::poll_override_error() == 0);
        }
    }

    #[test]
    fn authorize_privileged_success() {
        unsafe {
            magic::override_reset_state();
            magic::issue_override_code(2);
            let session = magic::poll_physical_override_privileged_session();
            assert!(session != (0 as *const c_void));
            magic::free_override_session(session);
            assert!(magic::poll_override_error() == 0);
        }
    }

    #[test]
    fn authorize_admin_success() {
        unsafe {
            magic::override_reset_state();
            magic::issue_override_code(3);
            let session = magic::poll_physical_override_admin_session();
            assert!(session != (0 as *const c_void));
            magic::free_override_session(session);
            assert!(magic::poll_override_error() == 0);
        }
    }
```

Deactivating active sessions

Deactivating active sessions is an error that attempts to authorize two sessions simultaneously, as follows:

```
    #[test]
    fn double_override_failure() {
        unsafe {
            magic::override_reset_state();
            magic::issue_override_code(1);
            magic::issue_override_code(1);
            assert!(magic::poll_override_session() == (0 as *const c_void));
            assert!(magic::poll_override_error() == 1);
        }
    }

    #[test]
```

```
fn double_privileged_failure() {
    unsafe {
        magic::override_reset_state();
        magic::issue_override_code(2);
        magic::issue_override_code(2);
        assert!(magic::poll_physical_override_privileged_session() == (0 as
*const c_void));
        assert!(magic::poll_override_error() == 1);
    }
}

#[test]
fn double_admin_failure() {
    unsafe {
        magic::override_reset_state();
        magic::issue_override_code(3);
        magic::issue_override_code(3);
        assert!(magic::poll_physical_override_admin_session() == (0 as *const
c_void));
        assert!(magic::poll_override_error() == 1);
    }
}
```

It is also disallowed to call a free session on the same object twice. Calling deconstructors in foreign libraries multiple times is highly discouraged due to possible memory corruption:

```
#[test]
fn double_free_override_failure() {
    unsafe {
        magic::override_reset_state();
        magic::issue_override_code(1);
        let session = magic::poll_override_session();
        assert!(session != (0 as *const c_void));
        magic::free_override_session(session);
        magic::free_override_session(session);
        assert!(magic::poll_override_error() == 2);
    }
}

#[test]
fn double_free_privileged_failure() {
    unsafe {
        magic::override_reset_state();
        magic::issue_override_code(2);
        let session = magic::poll_physical_override_privileged_session();
        assert!(session != (0 as *const c_void));
        magic::free_override_session(session);
        magic::free_override_session(session);
```

```
        assert!(magic::poll_override_error() == 2);
    }
}

#[test]
fn double_free_admin_failure() {
    unsafe {
        magic::override_reset_state();
        magic::issue_override_code(3);
        let session = magic::poll_physical_override_admin_session();
        assert!(session != (0 as *const c_void));
        magic::free_override_session(session);
        magic::free_override_session(session);
        assert!(magic::poll_override_error() == 2);
    }
}
```

Issuing normal commands

Normal commands do not require authorization, so these tests just check that the commands are issued and received:

```
#[test]
fn flash() {
    unsafe {
        magic::override_reset_state();
        magic::elevator_display_flash(222);
        assert!(magic::poll_override_code() == 7);
        assert!(magic::poll_override_code() == 222);
    }
}

#[test]
fn toggle_light() {
    unsafe {
        magic::override_reset_state();
        magic::elevator_display_toggle_light(33);
        assert!(magic::poll_override_code() == 8);
        assert!(magic::poll_override_code() == 33);
        assert!(magic::poll_override_code() == 1);
        magic::elevator_display_toggle_light(33);
        assert!(magic::poll_override_code() == 8);
        assert!(magic::poll_override_code() == 33);
        assert!(magic::poll_override_code() == 0);
    }
}
```

```
#[test]
fn set_light_color() {
    unsafe {
        magic::override_reset_state();
        magic::elevator_display_set_light_color(33, 222);
        assert!(magic::poll_override_code() == 9);
        assert!(magic::poll_override_code() == 33);
        assert!(magic::poll_override_code() == 222);
    }
}
```

Issuing privileged commands

Privileged commands will be allowed if there is an active authorized session:

```
#[test]
fn input_floor() {
    unsafe {
        magic::override_reset_state();
        magic::issue_override_code(3);
        magic::override_input_floor(2);
        assert!(magic::poll_override_code() == 4);
        assert!(magic::poll_override_code() == 2);
        assert!(magic::poll_override_error() == 0);
    }
}

#[test]
fn manual_mode() {
    unsafe {
        magic::override_reset_state();
        magic::issue_override_code(3);
        magic::override_manual_mode();
        assert!(magic::poll_override_code() == 5);
        assert!(magic::poll_override_error() == 0);
    }
}

#[test]
fn normal_mode() {
    unsafe {
        magic::override_reset_state();
        magic::issue_override_code(3);
        magic::override_normal_mode();
        assert!(magic::poll_override_code() == 6);
        assert!(magic::poll_override_error() == 0);
```

```
        }
    }
```

Denying unauthorized commands

Privileged commands will be denied if there is no active authorized session:

```
    #[test]
    fn deny_input_floor() {
        unsafe {
            magic::override_reset_state();
            magic::issue_override_code(4);
            magic::issue_override_code(2);
            assert!(magic::poll_override_error() == 3);
        }
    }

    #[test]
    fn deny_manual_mode() {
        unsafe {
            magic::override_reset_state();
            magic::issue_override_code(5);
            assert!(magic::poll_override_error() == 3);
        }
    }

    #[test]
    fn deny_normal_mode() {
        unsafe {
            magic::override_reset_state();
            magic::issue_override_code(6);
            assert!(magic::poll_override_error() == 3);
        }
    }
```

Inspecting the Rust tests

These tests in `src/tests/admin.rs` cover the high-level semantics defined in `src/admin.rs`. They cover mostly the same test cases as the lower level tests; however, some of these tests fail. To salvage the library, the library should be adjusted so that these tests will pass.

Rust authorization with sessions

Here are high-level tests covering the authentication and deactivation of sessions:

```rust
#[test]
fn authorize_override() {
    admin::reset_state();
    {
        let session = admin::authorize_override().ok();
        assert!(admin::is_override());
    }
    assert!(!admin::is_override());
    assert!(admin::check_error(()).is_ok());
}

#[test]
fn authorize_privileged() {
    admin::reset_state();
    {
        let session = admin::authorize_privileged().ok();
        assert(admin::is_privileged());
    }
    assert!(!admin::is_privileged());
    assert!(admin::check_error(()).is_ok());
}

#[test]
fn issue_admin_code() {
    admin::reset_state();
    {
        let session = admin::authorize_admin().ok();
        assert(admin::is_admin());
    }
    assert(!admin::is_admin());
    assert!(admin::check_error(()).is_ok());
}
```

Rust sharing session reference

The high-level library supports cloning sessions. Yikes! This could get complicated, but the tests are clear as to how it should work:

```rust
#[test]
fn clone_override() {
    admin::reset_state();
    {
        let session = admin::authorize_override().ok().unwrap();
        let session2 = session.clone();
        assert!(admin::is_override());
    }
    assert!(!admin::is_override());
    assert!(admin::check_error(()).is_ok());
}

#[test]
fn clone_privileged() {
    admin::reset_state();
    {
        let session = admin::authorize_privileged().ok().unwrap();
        let session2 = session.clone();
        assert!(admin::is_privileged());
    }
    assert!(!admin::is_privileged());
    assert!(admin::check_error(()).is_ok());
}

#[test]
fn clone_admin() {
    admin::reset_state();
    {
        let session = admin::authorize_admin().ok().unwrap();
        let session2 = session.clone();
        assert!(admin::is_admin());
    }
    assert!(!admin::is_admin());
    assert!(admin::check_error(()).is_ok());
}
```

Privileged commands

Privileged commands should be allowed if there is an active authorized session:

```
#[test]
fn input_floor() {
    admin::reset_state();
    {
        let session = admin::authorize_admin().ok();
        admin::input_floor(2).ok();
    }
    assert!(!admin::is_admin());
    assert!(admin::check_error(()).is_ok());
}

#[test]
fn manual_mode() {
    admin::reset_state();
    {
        let session = admin::authorize_admin().ok();
        admin::manual_mode().ok();
    }
    assert!(!admin::is_admin());
    assert!(admin::check_error(()).is_ok());
}

#[test]
fn normal_mode() {
    admin::reset_state();
    {
        let session = admin::authorize_admin().ok();
        admin::normal_mode().ok();
    }
    assert!(!admin::is_admin());
    assert!(admin::check_error(()).is_ok());
}
```

Unprivileged commands

Unprivileged commands should be allowed regardless of authentication:

```
#[test]
fn flash() {
    admin::reset_state();
    assert!(!admin::is_override());
    assert!(!admin::is_privileged());
    assert!(!admin::is_admin());
    admin::flash(222).ok();
    assert!(admin::check_error(()).is_ok());
}

#[test]
fn toggle_light() {
    admin::reset_state();
    assert!(!admin::is_override());
    assert!(!admin::is_privileged());
    assert!(!admin::is_admin());
    admin::toggle_light(7).ok();
    assert!(admin::check_error(()).is_ok());
}

#[test]
fn set_light_color() {
    admin::reset_state();
    assert!(!admin::is_override());
    assert!(!admin::is_privileged());
    assert!(!admin::is_admin());
    admin::set_light_color(33, 123).ok();
    assert!(admin::check_error(()).is_ok());
}
```

Denying access to privileged commands

Privileged commands should be denied if there is no authorized active session:

```
#[test]
fn deny_input_floor() {
    admin::reset_state();
    admin::input_floor(2).err();
    assert!(!admin::check_error(()).is_ok());
}

#[test]
```

```
fn deny_manual_mode() {
    admin::reset_state();
    admin::manual_mode().err();
    assert!(!admin::check_error(()).is_ok());
}

#[test]
fn deny_normal_mode() {
    admin::reset_state();
    admin::normal_mode().err();
    assert!(!admin::check_error(()).is_ok());
}
```

Learning the rules of ownership

Rust has three rules of ownership:

- Each value in Rust has a variable that's called its **owner**
- There can only be one owner at a time
- When the owner goes out of scope, the value will be dropped

In the simplest case, we can define a block with a variable that goes out of scope at the end of the block:

```
fn main()
{
    //variable x has not yet been defined
    {
        let x = 5;
        //variable x is now defined and owned by this context

        //variable x is going out of scope and will be dropped here
    }
    //variable x has gone out of scope and is no longer defined
}
```

We have brushed against the first two rules of ownership and lifetimes in previous chapters. However, this is the first chapter in which we have needed to work with the third rule—drop.

When the owner goes out of scope, the value will be dropped

In the preceding code, we can see the simple case where a function block is an owner. When the function block exits, the variables are dropped. Ownership can also be transferred, so when a value is sent or returned to another block, that block will become the new owner. The remaining case is that ownership is transferred to an object. When a value is dropped, all children objects are automatically dropped as well.

In the current project, there are three tests failing, all related to the `.clone` method on sessions. The failing sessions look like the following:

```
#[test]
fn clone_override() {
    admin::reset_state();
    {
        let session = admin::authorize_override().ok().unwrap();
        let session2 = session.clone();
        assert!(admin::is_override());
    }
    assert!(!admin::is_override());
    assert!(admin::check_error(()).is_ok());
}
```

Removing the boilerplate, we can see that each of the three tests follows the same pattern:

1. Open a new block
    1. Authorize a new session
    2. Clone the new session
    3. Confirm that session is authorized
2. Close the block
3. Confirm that session is not authorized
4. Confirm that no errors occurred

All tests work correctly, other than generating errors that are checked at the end of the test. The error code indicates a double free of the session. By normal Rust ownership rules, we know that cloned sessions will each be dropped individually. This makes sense because `Drop` is implemented for each of the two `AuthorizedSession` structs in scope. If we look at the implementation of `Drop` then we can see that it naively just calls the foreign library, which will cause the double free error:

```
#[derive(Clone)]
pub struct AuthorizedSession
{
    session: *const c_void
}
impl Drop for AuthorizedSession {
    fn drop(&mut self) {
        unsafe {
            magic::free_override_session(self.session);
        }
    }
}
```

Normally, Rust might complain about this careless resource management. However, the library uses an unsafe block to wrap the calls to the foreign function. Marking code as unsafe turns off many safety checks and encourages the compiler to trust the programmer. Calling foreign libraries is inherently unsafe, so this unsafe block is still necessary.

The correct behavior here seems to be to free the session only once after all cloned sessions have been dropped. This is a good case for `std::rc::Rc`, which stands for reference counted.

`Rc` works by storing one owned value internal to itself. All owners of an `Rc` no longer hold direct ownership over the inner object of the reference counted container. To use the inner object, the borrower must ask to borrow a pointer to the inner object. Ownership of `Rc` objects will be counted, and when all references containing a given value are gone, the value will be dropped.

This built-in functionality provides exactly what we want. Clone multiple times, drop once, as follows:

```
struct AuthorizedSessionInner(*const c_void);

#[derive(Clone)]
pub struct AuthorizedSession
{
    session: Rc<AuthorizedSessionInner>
}
```

```
impl Drop for AuthorizedSessionInner {
    fn drop(&mut self) {
        unsafe {
            magic::free_override_session(self.0);
        }
    }
}
```

To initialize sessions from raw pointers, we need to wrap them. Otherwise, no code needs to change:

```
let session = AuthorizedSession {
    session: Rc::new(AuthorizedSessionInner(session))
};
```

After these small changes, the three remaining tests pass. The library seems to be working. The big lesson to learn here is that `Drop` implementations can be very sensitive sometimes. Don't assume that multiple drops will be safe. To deal with complex situations, we have in the standard library the types `std::rc::Rc` and `std::sync::Arc`. `Arc` is a threadsafe version of `Rc`.

Using immutable data

After implementing and testing the library with real elevators, you find another bug—when someone physically keys into a session, sometimes they get deauthorized while still using the elevator. Sometimes is a terrible word to hear in a bug report.

Fixing the hard-to-reproduce bug

After way too much searching and researching, you find a test case that reliably reproduces the problem:

```
#[test]
fn invalid_deauthorization() {
    admin::reset_state();
    let session = admin::authorize_admin().ok();
    assert!(admin::authorize_admin().is_err());
    assert!(admin::is_admin());
}
```

Looking at this test case, the first thing we might ask is, why should this be permitted?

The problem that we encountered during physical testing was characterized by the random deauthorization of valid sessions. What was discovered during investigations was that during physically authorized sessions, sometimes software authorized sessions would be initiated. A physical authorization is when someone uses a key on the elevator to use special commands. Software authorization is any other authorized session initiated from the running software, rather than from the elevator hardware. This double authorization action violated the double authorization constraint, so both sessions were invalidated. The resolution is clearly to permit the first authorized session to continue, while rejecting the second authorization.

The solution seems fairly direct and straightforward. From `src/admin.rs`, we have the ability to check whether any session is authorized from the library, then reject the second authorization without calling the library.

So, rewriting the authorize commands, we add a check to see whether there is already an authorized session. If such a session exists, then this authorization fails:

```
pub fn authorize_override() -> Result<AuthorizedSession,ErrorCode>
{
   if is_override() || is_privileged() || is_admin() {
      return Result::Err(ErrorCode::DoubleAuthorize)
   }
   let session = unsafe {
      magic::issue_override_code(OverrideCode::IssueOverride as i32);
      magic::poll_override_session()
   };
   let session = AuthorizedSession {
      session: Rc::new(AuthorizedSessionInner(session))
   };
   check_error(session)
}

pub fn authorize_privileged() -> Result<AuthorizedSession,ErrorCode>
{ ... }

pub fn authorize_admin() -> Result<AuthorizedSession,ErrorCode>
{ ... }
```

This change fixes the immediate problem, but causes the double free tests to fail, because now there is no error code generated from the library after double free. We are essentially protecting the underlying library from double free responsibility, so this is a foreseeable consequence. The new tests just remove the last line that previously checked for the error code:

```
#[test]
fn double_override_failure() {
    admin::reset_state();
    let session = admin::authorize_override().ok();
    assert!(admin::authorize_override().err().is_some());
}

#[test]
fn double_privileged_failure() {
    admin::reset_state();
    let session = admin::authorize_privileged().ok();
    assert!(admin::authorize_privileged().err().is_some());
}

#[test]
fn double_admin_failure() {
    admin::reset_state();
    let session = admin::authorize_admin().ok();
    assert!(admin::authorize_admin().err().is_some());
}
```

Preventing hard-to-reproduce bugs

Rust was specifically designed to avoid hard-to-reproduce bugs like this. Raw pointer handling is prevented or strongly discouraged in Rust. A raw pointer is like a reference that Rust knows nothing about, and therefore can provide no safety guarantees regarding its use. Unfortunately, this bug is internal to a foreign library, so our Rust project doesn't have jurisdiction to complain about the root problem here. Despite this, there are still good practices that we can follow to prevent or limit the occurrence of bugs related to mutation and strange side-effects.

The first technique we will recommend is immutability. By default, all variables are declared as immutable. This is Rust's way of not so subtly telling you to avoid mutating values if possible, as follows:

```
fn main() {
    let a = 5;
    let mut b = 5;

    //a = 4; not valid
    b = 4;

    //*(&mut a) = 3; not valid
    *(&mut b) = 3;
}
```

Immutable values cannot be borrowed as mutable (by design), so requiring mutability for a function parameter will require mutability from each value sent to it:

```
fn f(x: &mut i32) {
    *x = 2;
}

fn main() {
    let a = 5;
    let mut b = 5;

    //f(&mut a); not valid
    f(&mut b);
}
```

Turning an immutable value into a mutable one can be as simple as cloning it to create a new identical value; however, as we have seen throughout this chapter, the clone is not always a simple operation, an example is shown as follows:

```
use std::sync::{Mutex, Arc};

#[derive(Clone)]
struct TimeBomb {
    countdown: Arc<Mutex<i32>>
}
impl Drop for TimeBomb
{
    fn drop(&mut self) {
        let mut c = self.countdown.lock().unwrap();
        *c -= 1;
        if *c <= 0 {
            panic!("BOOM!!")
```

```
        }
      }
    }

fn main()
{
    let t3 = TimeBomb {
        countdown: Arc::new(Mutex::new(3))
    };
    let t2 = t3.clone();
    let t1 = t2.clone();
    let t0 = t1.clone();
}
```

Declaring a variable as immutable does not absolutely prevent all mutation, inside or out. In Rust, immutable variables are permitted to hold interior fields with datatypes that are mutable. For example, `std::cell::RefCell` can be used to achieve interior mutability over whatever data it holds.

Despite the exceptions, using immutable by default variables can help prevent simple bugs from becoming complex bugs. Don't let your programming style become a liability; practice defensive software development.

Using pure functions

Pure functions are the second technique that we recommend to prevent hard-to-reproduce bugs. Pure functions can be thought of as an extension of the avoid side-effects principle. The definition of a pure function is a function where the following is true:

- No changes are caused outside of the function (no side-effects)
- The return value does not depend on anything but the function parameters

Here are some examples of pure functions:

```
fn p0() {}

fn p1() -> u64 {
    444
}

fn p2(x: u64) -> u64 {
    x * 444
}
```

```
fn p3(x: u64, y: u64) -> u64 {
   x * 444 + y
}

fn main()
{
   p0();
   p1();
   p2(3);
   p3(3,4);
}
```

Here are some examples of impure functions:

```
use std::cell::Cell;

static mut blah: u64 = 3;
fn ip0() {
   unsafe {
      blah = 444;
   }
}

fn ip1(c: &Cell<u64>) {
   c.set(333);
}

fn main()
{
   ip0();
   let r = Cell::new(3);
   ip1(&r);
   ip1(&r);
}
```

Rust does not have any language feature that specifically designates a function as more or less pure. However, as the preceding examples illustrate, Rust somewhat discourages impure functions. Function purity should be regarded as a design pattern and is strongly associated with the good functional style.

Closures can also be pure or impure in the same fashion as top-level functions. As such, function purity becomes a concern when working with higher-level functions. Certain patterns of functional programming expect functions to be pure. A good example is the memoization pattern that we briefly mentioned in Chapter 1, *Functional Programming – a Comparison*. Let's compare what can happen to memoization if the memoized function is impure.

First, here is a reminder of how memoization is supposed to work:

```
#[macro_use] extern crate cached;

cached!{
    FIB;
    fn fib(n: u64) -> u64 = {
        if n == 0 || n == 1 { return n }
        fib(n-1) + fib(n-2)
    }
}

fn main() {
    fib(30); //call 1, generates correct value and returns it
    fib(30); //call 2, finds correct value and returns it
}
```

Next, let's look at a memoized impure function:

```
#[macro_use] extern crate lazy_static;
#[macro_use] extern crate cached;
use std::collections::HashMap;
use std::sync::Mutex;

lazy_static! {
    static ref BUCKET_COUNTER: Mutex<HashMap<u64, u64>> = {
        Mutex::new(HashMap::new())
    };
}

cached!{
    BUCK;
    fn bucket_count(n: u64) -> u64 = {
        let mut counter = BUCKET_COUNTER.lock().unwrap();
        let r = match counter.get(&n) {
            Some(c) => { c+1 }
            None => { 1 }
        };
        counter.insert(n, r);
        r
    }
}

fn main() {
    bucket_count(30); //call 1, generates correct value and returns it
    bucket_count(30); //call 2, finds stale value and returns it
}
```

This first cache example should return the same value every time. The second example should not return the same value every time. Semantically, we don't want the second example to return stale values; however, this also means that we cannot safely cache the results. There is a necessary performance trade-off. There is nothing wrong with the purity or impurity of either example here if it is necessary. It just means that the second example should not be cached.

However, there are also anti-patterns of impurity. Let's look at another impure function that behaves poorly:

```
#[macro_use] extern crate cached;
use std::sync::{Arc,Mutex};

#[derive(Clone)]
pub struct TimeBomb {
    countdown: Arc<Mutex<i32>>
}

impl Drop for TimeBomb
{
    fn drop(&mut self) {
        let mut c = self.countdown.lock().unwrap();
        *c -= 1;
        if *c <= 0 {
            panic!("BOOM!!")
        }
    }
}

cached!{
    TICKING_BOX;
    fn tick_tock(v: i32) -> TimeBomb = {
        TimeBomb {
            countdown: Arc::new(Mutex::new(v))
        }
    }
}

fn main() {
    tick_tock(3);
    tick_tock(3);
    tick_tock(3);
}
```

In this example, the data itself is impure. Every `tick_tock` moves and drops a `TimeBomb`. Eventually, it explodes and our cache doesn't help to protect us. Hopefully, you won't need to work with bombshells in your programs.

Summary

In this chapter, we worked with legacy code and foreign libraries in Rust. Rust safeguards can be annoying to learn and sometimes burdensome to work with, but the alternative of fast and loose coding is also stressful and problematic.

One of the motivations for Rust memory safety rules is the concept of double free memory, which we mentioned in this chapter. However, the code presented did not involve a real double free of memory. A real double free causes something known as undefined behavior. Undefined behavior is a term used in language standards to refer to operations that will cause the program to act strangely. Double freed memory is typically one of the worst types of undefined behavior, causing memory corruption and subsequent crashes or invalid states that are hard to trace back to the original cause.

In the latter half of the chapter, we examined specific Rust design decisions, features, and patterns such as ownership, immutability, and pure functions. These are Rust's defense mechanisms against undefined behavior and other ills.

Using Rust safeguards correctly and not circumventing them has many benefits. Rust encourages a certain style of programming that benefits the design of larger projects. Typically, project architecture follows a more-than-linear bug/complexity curve. As a project grows in size, the number of bugs and difficult situations will grow at an even faster rate. By locking down common sources of bugs or code dependency, it is possible to develop large projects with fewer problems.

In the next chapter, we will formally explain many functional design patterns. This will be a good opportunity to learn the extent to which functional programming principles apply and are relevant to Rust. If nothing in the next chapter seems cool or useful, then the author has failed.

Questions

1. What does `Rc` stand for?
2. What does `Arc` stand for?
3. What is a weak reference?
4. Which superpowers are enabled in unsafe blocks?
5. When will an object be dropped?
6. What is the difference between lifetimes and ownership?
7. How can you be sure that a function is safe?
8. What is memory corruption and how would it affect a program?

7
Design Patterns

Functional programming has developed design patterns just like object-oriented or other communities. These patterns, unsurprisingly, make use of functions as a central concept. They also emphasize something called the **single responsibility principle**. The single responsibility principle states that program's logical components should do one thing and do that one thing well. In this chapter, we will focus on a few very common patterns. Some of these concepts are so simple that they counter-intuitively become harder to explain. In these cases, we will make use of various examples to demonstrate how a simple concept can exhibit complex behavior.

In this chapter, you will do the following:

- Learn to recognize and use functors
- Learn to recognize and use monads
- Learn to recognize and use combinators
- Learn to recognize and use lazy evaluation

Technical requirements

A recent version of Rust is necessary to run the examples provided:

https://www.rust-lang.org/en-US/install.html

This chapter's code is also available on GitHub:

https://github.com/PacktPublishing/Hands-On-Functional-Programming-in-RUST

Specific installation and build instructions are also included in each chapter's README.md file.

Using the functor pattern

A functor is approximately the inverse of a function:

- A function defines a transformation, accepts data, and returns the result of the transformation
- A functor defines data, accepts a function, and returns the result of the transformation

A simple example of a functor is the Rust vector and its accompanying map function:

```
fn main() {
    let m: Vec<u64> = vec![1, 2, 3];
    let n: Vec<u64> = m.iter().map(|x| { x*x }).collect();
    println!("{:?}", m);
    println!("{:?}", n);
}
```

Functors are often thought of as only the map function, due to the rules of what constitutes a functor or not. The preceding common case is what's called a **structure-preserving map**. Functors do not need to be structure-preserving. For example, take the very similar case of a map implemented for a set, as shown in the following code:

```
use std::collections::{HashSet};

fn main() {
    let mut a: HashSet<u64> = HashSet::new();
    a.insert(1);
    a.insert(2);
    a.insert(3);
    a.insert(4);
    let b: HashSet<u64> = a.iter().cloned().map(|x| x/2).collect();
    println!("{:?}", a);
    println!("{:?}", b);
}
```

We see here that the resulting set is smaller than the original set due to collisions. This mapping still satisfies the properties of a functor. The defining properties of a functor are as follows:

- A collection of objects, C
- A mapping function that will transform objects in C into objects in D

The preceding `Set` map satisfies both the first and second property, and is therefore a proper functor. It also demonstrates how data can be transformed into a differently shaped structure through a functor. Using a little imagination, we may also consider the case where each mapped value may produce multiple outputs:

```
fn main() {
    let sentences = vec!["this is a sentence","paragraphs have many
sentences"];
    let words:Vec<&str> = sentences.iter().flat_map(|&x| x.split("
")).collect();
    println!("{:?}", sentences);
    println!("{:?}", words);
}
```

Technically speaking, this last case is not a normal functor, but rather a contravariant functor. All functors are covariant. The distinction between covariance and contravariance is not important for our purposes, so we will leave that topic to only the most curious readers.

As a final definition by example, we should note that the input and output of a functor map need not be of the same type. For example, we can map from a vector to a `HashSet`:

```
use std::collections::{HashSet};

fn main() {
    let v: Vec<u64> = vec![1, 2, 3];
    let s: HashSet<u64> = v.iter().cloned().map(|x| x/2).collect();
    println!("{:?}", v);
    println!("{:?}", s);
}
```

To give a non-trivial example of how the functor pattern could be used, let's look at webcams and AI. Modern AI facial recognition software is capable of identifying human faces in pictures and even visible emotional states. Let's imagine an app that connects to a webcam and processes the input with a filter. Here are some type definitions for the program:

```
struct WebCamera;

#[derive(Debug)]
enum VisibleEmotion {
    Anger,
    Contempt,
    Disgust,
    Fear,
    Happiness,
```

```
        Neutral,
        Sadness,
        Surprise
    }

    #[derive(Debug,Clone)]
    struct BoundingBox {
        top: u64,
        left: u64,
        height: u64,
        width: u64
    }

    #[derive(Debug)]
    enum CameraFilters {
        Sparkles,
        Rain,
        Fire,
        Disco
    }
```

On the `WebCamera` type, we will implement two functors. One functor, `map_emotion`, will map emotions to other emotions. Maybe this could be used to add emojis to the text chat. The second contravariant functor, `flatmap_emotion`, maps emotions to zero, or more filters. These are animations or effects that can be applied back onto the web camera field of view:

```
    impl WebCamera {
        fn map_emotion<T,F>(&self, translate: F) -> Vec<(BoundingBox,T)>
        where F: Fn(VisibleEmotion) -> T {
            //Simulate emotion extracted from WebCamera
            vec![
                (BoundingBox { top: 1, left: 1, height: 1, width: 1 },
    VisibleEmotion::Anger),
                (BoundingBox { top: 1, left: 1, height: 1, width: 1 },
    VisibleEmotion::Sadness),
                (BoundingBox { top: 4, left: 4, height: 1, width: 1 },
    VisibleEmotion::Surprise),
                (BoundingBox { top: 8, left: 1, height: 1, width: 1 },
    VisibleEmotion::Neutral)
            ].into_iter().map(|(bb,emt)| {
                (bb, translate(emt))
            }).collect::<Vec<(BoundingBox,T)>>()
        }
        fn flatmap_emotion<T,F,U:IntoIterator<Item=T>>(&self, mut translate:
    F) -> Vec<(BoundingBox,T)>
```

```
    where F: FnMut(VisibleEmotion) -> U {
        //Simulate emotion extracted from WebCamera
        vec![
            (BoundingBox { top: 1, left: 1, height: 1, width: 1 },
VisibleEmotion::Anger),
            (BoundingBox { top: 1, left: 1, height: 1, width: 1 },
VisibleEmotion::Sadness),
            (BoundingBox { top: 4, left: 4, height: 1, width: 1 },
VisibleEmotion::Surprise),
            (BoundingBox { top: 8, left: 1, height: 1, width: 1 },
VisibleEmotion::Neutral)
        ].into_iter().flat_map(|(bb,emt)| {
            translate(emt).into_iter().map(move |t| (bb.clone(), t))
        }).collect::<Vec<(BoundingBox,T)>>()
    }
}
```

To use the functors, the programmer supplies which emotions map to which filters. The complex AI and effects can be easily modified due to the encapsulation provided by the functor pattern:

```
fn main() {
    let camera = WebCamera;
    let emotes: Vec<(BoundingBox,VisibleEmotion)> =
camera.map_emotion(|emt| {
        match emt {
            VisibleEmotion::Anger |
            VisibleEmotion::Contempt |
            VisibleEmotion::Disgust |
            VisibleEmotion::Fear |
            VisibleEmotion::Sadness => VisibleEmotion::Happiness,
            VisibleEmotion::Neutral |
            VisibleEmotion::Happiness |
            VisibleEmotion::Surprise => VisibleEmotion::Sadness
        }
    });

    let filters: Vec<(BoundingBox,CameraFilters)> =
camera.flatmap_emotion(|emt| {
        match emt {
            VisibleEmotion::Anger |
            VisibleEmotion::Contempt |
            VisibleEmotion::Disgust |
            VisibleEmotion::Fear |
            VisibleEmotion::Sadness => vec![CameraFilters::Sparkles,
CameraFilters::Rain],
            VisibleEmotion::Neutral |
```

```
                VisibleEmotion::Happiness |
                VisibleEmotion::Surprise => vec![CameraFilters::Disco]
        }
    });

    println!("{:?}",emotes);
    println!("{:?}",filters);
}
```

Using the monad pattern

A monad defines `return` and `bind` operations for a type. The `return` operation is like a constructor to make the monad. The `bind` operation incorporates new information and returns a new monad. There are also several laws that monads should obey. Rather than quote the laws, we'll just say that monads should behave well when daisy chained like the following:

```
MyMonad::return(value)   //We start with a new MyMonad<A>
        .bind(|x| x+x)   //We take a step into MyMonad<B>
        .bind(|y| y*y);  //Similarly we get to MyMonad<C>
```

In Rust, there are several semi-monads that appear in standard libraries:

```
fn main()
{
    let v1 = Some(2).and_then(|x| Some(x+x)).and_then(|y| Some(y*y));
    println!("{:?}", v1);

    let v2 = None.or_else(|| None).or_else(|| Some(222));
    println!("{:?}", v2);
}
```

In this example, the normal `Option` constructors, `Some` or `None`, take the place of the monadic naming convention, `return`. There are two semi-monads implemented here, one associated with `and_then`, and the other with `or_else`. Both of these correspond to the monadic `bind` naming convention for the operator responsible for incorporating new information into a new monad return value.

Monadic `bind` operations are also polymorphic, meaning they should permit returning monads of different types from the current monad. According to this rule, `or_else` is not technically a monad; hence it is a semi-monad:

```
fn main() {
    let v3 = Some(2).and_then(|x| Some("abc"));
    println!("{:?}", v3);

    // or_else is not quite a monad
    // does not permit polymorphic bind
    //let v4 = Some(2).or_else(|| Some("abc"));
    //println!("{:?}", v4);
}
```

Monads were originally developed to express side-effects in purely functional languages. Isn't that a contradiction—pure with side-effects?

The answer is *no* if the effects are passed as input and output through pure functions. However, for this to work, every function would need to declare every state variable and pass it along, which could become a huge list of parameters. This is where monads come in. A monad can hide state inside itself, which becomes essentially a larger, more complex function than what the programmer interacts with.

One concrete example of side-effect hiding is the concept of a universal logger. The monadic `return` and `bind` can be used to wrap state and computation inside of a monad that will log all intermediate results. Here is the logger monad:

```
use std::fmt::{Debug};

struct LogMonad<T>(T);
impl<T> LogMonad<T> {
    fn _return(t: T) -> LogMonad<T>
    where T: Debug {
        println!("{:?}", t);
        LogMonad(t)
    }
    fn bind<R,F>(&self, f: F) -> LogMonad<R>
    where F: FnOnce(&T) -> R,
    R: Debug {
        let r = f(&self.0);
        println!("{:?}", r);
        LogMonad(r)
    }
}

fn main() {
```

```
LogMonad::_return(4)
        .bind(|x| x+x)
        .bind(|y| y*y)
        .bind(|z| format!("{}{}{}", z, z, z));
}
```

As long as each result implements the `Debug` trait, it can be automatically logged with this pattern.

The monad pattern is also very useful for chaining together code that can't be written in a normal code block. For example, code blocks are always evaluated eagerly. If you want to define code that will be evaluated later or in pieces, the lazy monad pattern is very convenient. Lazy evaluation is a term used to describe code or data that is not evaluated until it is referenced. This is contrary to the typical eager evaluation of Rust code that will execute immediately regardless of context. Here is the lazy monad pattern:

```
struct LazyMonad<A,B>(Box<Fn(A) -> B>);

impl<A: 'static,B: 'static> LazyMonad<A,B> {
   fn _return(u: A) -> LazyMonad<B,B> {
      LazyMonad(Box::new(move |b: B| b))
   }
   fn bind<C,G: 'static>(self, g: G) -> LazyMonad<A,C>
   where G: Fn(B) -> C {
      LazyMonad(Box::new(move |a: A| g(self.0(a))))
   }
   fn apply(self, a: A) -> B {
      self.0(a)
   }
}

fn main() {
   let notyet = LazyMonad::_return(())   //we create LazyMonad<()>
                       .bind(|x| x+2) //and now a LazyMonad<A>
                       .bind(|y| y*3) //and now a LazyMonad<B>
                       .bind(|z| format!("{}{}", z, z));

   let nowdoit = notyet.apply(222); //The above code now run
   println!("nowdoit {}", nowdoit);
}
```

This block defines statements that will be evaluated one at a time after a value is supplied, but not before. This may seem a bit trivial since we can do the same with a simple closure and code block; however, to make this pattern stick, let's consider a more complex case—an asynchronous web server.

A web server will typically receive a full HTTP request before processing it. Choosing what to do with a request is sometimes called **routing**. Then requests are sent to a request handler. In the following code, we define a server that helps us wrap routes and handlers into a single web server object. Here are the type and method definitions:

```
use std::io::prelude::*;
use std::net::TcpListener;
use std::net::TcpStream;

struct ServerMonad<St> {
    state: St,
    handlers: Vec<Box<Fn(&mut St,&String) -> Option<String>>>
}

impl<St: Clone> ServerMonad<St> {
    fn _return(st: St) -> ServerMonad<St> {
        ServerMonad {
            state: st,
            handlers: Vec::new()
        }
    }
    fn listen(&mut self, address: &str) {
        let listener = TcpListener::bind(address).unwrap();
        for stream in listener.incoming() {
            let mut st = self.state.clone();
            let mut buffer = [0; 2048];
            let mut tcp = stream.unwrap();
            tcp.read(&mut buffer);
            let buffer = String::from_utf8_lossy(&buffer).into_owned();
            for h in self.handlers.iter() {
                if let Some(response) = h(&mut st,&buffer) {
                    tcp.write(response.as_bytes());
                    break
                }
            }
        }
    }
    fn bind_handler<F>(mut self, f: F) -> Self
        where F: 'static + Fn(&mut St,&String) -> Option<String> {
        self.handlers.push(Box::new(f));
        self
    }
}
```

This type defines `return` and `bind` like operations. However, the `bind` function is not polymorphic and the operation is not a pure function. Without these compromises, we would need to fight against the Rust type and ownership system; the preceding example is not written monadically due to complications when trying to box and copy closures. This is an expected trade-off and the semi-monad pattern should not be discouraged when appropriate.

To define our web server responses, we can attach handlers like in the following code:

```
fn main() {
    ServerMonad::_return(())
                    .bind_handler(|&mut st, ref msg| if msg.len()%2 == 0 {
Some("divisible by 2".to_string()) } else { None })
                    .bind_handler(|&mut st, ref msg| if msg.len()%3 == 0 {
Some("divisible by 3".to_string()) } else { None })
                    .bind_handler(|&mut st, ref msg| if msg.len()%5 == 0 {
Some("divisible by 5".to_string()) } else { None })
                    .bind_handler(|&mut st, ref msg| if msg.len()%7 == 0 {
Some("divisible by 7".to_string()) } else { None })
                    .listen("127.0.0.1:8888");
}
```

If you run this program and send messages to localhost 8888, then you may get a response if the message length is divisible by 2, 3, 5, or 7.

Using the combinator pattern

A combinator is a function that takes other functions as arguments and returns a new function.

A simple example of a combinator would be the composition operator, which chains two functions together:

```
fn compose<A,B,C,F,G>(f: F, g: G) -> impl Fn(A) -> C
    where F: 'static + Fn(A) -> B,
          G: 'static + Fn(B) -> C {
    move |x| g(f(x))
}

fn main() {
    let fa = |x| x+1;
    let fb = |y| y*2;
    let fc = |z| z/3;
    let g = compose(compose(fa,fb),fc);
```

```
        println!("g(1) = {}", g(1));
        println!("g(12) = {}", g(12));
        println!("g(123) = {}", g(123));
    }
```

Parser combinators

Another major application of combinators is parser combinators. A parser combinator makes use of both the monad and combinator patterns. The monadic `bind` functions are used to bind data from parsers that are later returned as a parse result. The combinators join parsers into a sequence, failover, or other patterns.

The `chomp` parser combinator library is a good implementation of this concept. Also, the library provides a nice `parse!` macro that makes the combinator logic much easier to read. Here is an example:

```rust
#[macro_use]
extern crate chomp;
use chomp::prelude::*;

#[derive(Debug, Eq, PartialEq)]
struct Name<B: Buffer> {
    first: B,
    last:  B,
}

fn name<I: U8Input>(i: I) -> SimpleResult<I, Name<I::Buffer>> {
    parse!{i;
        let first = take_while1(|c| c != b' ');
        token(b' ');  // skipping this char
        let last  = take_while1(|c| c != b'\n');

        ret Name{
            first: first,
            last:  last,
        }
    }
}

fn main() {
    let parse_result = parse_only(name, "Martin
Wernstål\n".as_bytes()).unwrap();
    println!("first:{} last:{}",
```

```
        String::from_utf8_lossy(parse_result.first),
        String::from_utf8_lossy(parse_result.last));
}
```

Here, the example defines a grammar for a first name, last name parser. In the name function, the parser is defined with a macro. The inside of the macro looks almost like a normal code, like the `let` statements, function calls, and closure definitions. However, the generated code is actually a mix of monads and combinators.

Each `let` binding corresponds to a combinator. Each semicolon corresponds to a combinator. The functions `take_while1` and `token` are both combinators that introduce parser monads. Then, when the macro ends, we are left with an expression that processes the input to parse a result.

This `chomp` parser combinator library is fully featured and may be hard to understand if you just casually examined the source code. To see what is happening here, let's create our own parser combinators. First, let's define the parser state:

```
use std::rc::Rc;

#[derive(Clone)]
struct ParseState<A: Clone> {
    buffer: Rc<Vec<char>>,
    index: usize,
    a: A
}

impl<A: Clone> ParseState<A> {
    fn new(a: A, buffer: String) -> ParseState<A> {
        let buffer: Vec<char> = buffer.chars().collect();
        ParseState {
            buffer: Rc::new(buffer),
            index: 0,
            a: a
        }
    }
    fn next(&self) -> (ParseState<A>,Option<char>) {
        if self.index < self.buffer.len() {
            let new_char = self.buffer[self.index];
            let new_index = self.index + 1;
            (ParseState {
                buffer: Arc::clone(&self.buffer),
                index: new_index,
                a: self.a.clone()
            }, Some(new_char))
        } else {
```

```
                (ParseState {
                    buffer: Rc::clone(&self.buffer),
                    index: self.index,
                    a: self.a.clone()
                },None)
            }
        }
    }

    #[derive(Debug)]
    struct ParseRCon<A,B>(A,Result<Option<B>,String>);

    #[derive(Debug)]
    enum ParseOutput<A> {
        Success(A),
        Failure(String)
    }
```

Here we define `ParseState`, `ParseRCon`, and `ParseResult`. The parse state keeps track of what character index the parser is at. The parse state often also records information, such as the line and column number.

The `ParseRCon` structure encapsulates state along with an optional value wrapped in a result. If an unrecoverable error happens while parsing, the result will become `Err`. If a recoverable error happens while parsing, the option will be `None`. Otherwise, the parsers should work mostly as if they expect to always have the optional value.

The `ParseResult` type is returned at the very end of a parse execution to provide a successful result or error message.

The parser monads and combinators are defined ad hoc with different functions. To create a parser, the simplest options would be `parse_mzero` and `parse_return`:

```
    fn parse<St: Clone,A,P>(p: &P, st: &ParseState<St>) -> ParseOutput<A>
        where P: Fn(ParseState<St>) -> ParseRCon<ParseState<St>,A> {
        match p(st.clone()) {
            ParseRCon(_,Ok(Some(a))) => ParseOutput::Success(a),
            ParseRCon(_,Ok(None)) => ParseOutput::Failure("expected
    input".to_string()),
            ParseRCon(_,Err(err)) => ParseOutput::Failure(err)
        }
    }

    fn parse_mzero<St: Clone,A>(st: ParseState<St>) ->
    ParseRCon<ParseState<St>,A> {
        ParseRCon(st,Err("mzero failed".to_string()))
```

```
    }

    fn parse_return<St: Clone,A: Clone>(a: A) -> impl (Fn(ParseState<St>)
    -> ParseRCon<ParseState<St>,A>) {
        move |st| { ParseRCon(st,Ok(Some(a.clone()))) }
    }

    fn main() {
        let input1 = ParseState::new((), "1 + 2 * 3".to_string());
        let input2 = ParseState::new((), "3 / 2 - 1".to_string());

        let p1 = parse_mzero::<(),()>;
        println!("p1 input1: {:?}", parse(&p1,&input1));
        println!("p1 input2: {:?}", parse(&p1,&input2));

        let p2 = parse_return(123);
        println!("p2 input1: {:?}", parse(&p2,&input1));
        println!("p2 input2: {:?}", parse(&p2,&input2));
    }
```

The parse_mzero monad always fails and returns a simple message. The parse_return always succeeds and returns a given value.

To make things more interesting, let's actually look at a parser that consumes input. We create the following two functions—parse_token and parse_satisfy. parse_token will always consume one token and return its value unless there is no more input. parse_satisfy will consume a token if the token satisfies some condition. Here are the definitions:

```
    fn parse_token<St: Clone,A,T>(t: T) -> impl (Fn(ParseState<St>) ->
    ParseRCon<ParseState<St>,A>)
        where T: 'static + Fn(char) -> Option<A> {
        move |st: ParseState<St>| {
            let (next_state,next_char) = st.clone().next();
            match next_char {
                Some(c) => ParseRCon(next_state,Ok(t(c))),
                None => ParseRCon(st,Err("end of input".to_string()))
            }
        }
    }

    fn parse_satisfy<St: Clone,T>(t: T) -> impl (Fn(ParseState<St>) ->
    ParseRCon<ParseState<St>,char>)
        where T: 'static + Fn(char) -> bool {
        parse_token(move |c| if t(c) {Some(c)} else {None})
    }
```

```
fn main() {
    let input1 = ParseState::new((), "1 + 2 * 3".to_string());
    let input2 = ParseState::new((), "3 / 2 - 1".to_string());

    let p3 = parse_satisfy(|c| c=='1');
    println!("p3 input1: {:?}", parse(&p3,&input1));
    println!("p3 input2: {:?}", parse(&p3,&input2));

    let digit = parse_satisfy(|c| c.is_digit(10));
    println!("digit input1: {:?}", parse(&digit,&input1));
    println!("digit input2: {:?}", parse(&digit,&input2));

    let space = parse_satisfy(|c| c==' ');
    println!("space input1: {:?}", parse(&space,&input1));
    println!("space input2: {:?}", parse(&space,&input2));

    let operator = parse_satisfy(|c| c=='+' || c=='-' || c=='*' ||
c=='/');
    println!("operator input1: {:?}", parse(&operator,&input1));
    println!("operator input2: {:?}", parse(&operator,&input2));
}
```

The `parse_token` and `parse_satisfy` look at one token. If the token satisfies the provided condition, it then returns the input token. Here, we create several conditions to correspond to single character matching, digits, spaces, or arithmetic operators.

These functions can be composed using high-level combinators to create complex grammar:

```
fn parse_bind<St: Clone,A,B,P1,P2,B1>(p1: P1, b1: B1)
    -> impl Fn(ParseState<St>) -> ParseRCon<ParseState<St>,B>
    where P1: Fn(ParseState<St>) -> ParseRCon<ParseState<St>,A>,
          P2: Fn(ParseState<St>) -> ParseRCon<ParseState<St>,B>,
          B1: Fn(A) -> P2 {
    move |st| {
        match p1(st) {
            ParseRCon(nst,Ok(Some(a))) => b1(a)(nst),
            ParseRCon(nst,Ok(None)) => ParseRCon(nst,Err("bind
failed".to_string())),
            ParseRCon(nst,Err(err)) => ParseRCon(nst,Err(err))
        }
    }
}

fn parse_sequence<St: Clone,A,B,P1,P2>(p1: P1, p2: P2)
    -> impl Fn(ParseState<St>) -> ParseRCon<ParseState<St>,B>
    where P1: Fn(ParseState<St>) -> ParseRCon<ParseState<St>,A>,
          P2: Fn(ParseState<St>) -> ParseRCon<ParseState<St>,B> {
```

```
      move |st| {
         match p1(st) {
            ParseRCon(nst,Ok(_)) => p2(nst),
            ParseRCon(nst,Err(err)) => ParseRCon(nst,Err(err))
         }
      }
   }

fn parse_or<St: Clone,A,P1,P2>(p1: P1, p2: P2)
   -> impl Fn(ParseState<St>) -> ParseRCon<ParseState<St>,A>
   where P1: Fn(ParseState<St>) -> ParseRCon<ParseState<St>,A>,
         P2: Fn(ParseState<St>) -> ParseRCon<ParseState<St>,A> {
   move |st| {
      match p1(st.clone()) {
         ParseRCon(nst,Ok(Some(a))) => ParseRCon(nst,Ok(Some(a))),
         ParseRCon(_,Ok(None)) => p2(st),
         ParseRCon(nst,Err(err)) => ParseRCon(nst,Err(err))
      }
   }
}

fn main() {
   let input1 = ParseState::new((), "1 + 2 * 3".to_string());
   let input2 = ParseState::new((), "3 / 2 - 1".to_string());

   let digit = parse_satisfy(|c| c.is_digit(10));
   let space = parse_satisfy(|c| c==' ');
   let operator = parse_satisfy(|c| c=='+' || c=='-' || c=='*' ||
c=='/');
   let ps1 = parse_sequence(digit,space);
   let ps2 = parse_sequence(ps1,operator);
   println!("digit,space,operator input1: {:?}", parse(&ps2,&input1));
   println!("digit,space,operator input2: {:?}", parse(&ps2,&input2));
}
```

Here, we see how the monadic `parse_bind` or its derivative, `parse_sequence`, can be used to sequence two parsers together. We don't have an example here but the failover combinator is also defined in `parse_or`.

Using these primitives, we can create nice tools to help us generate complex parsers that expect, store, and manipulate data from token streams. Parse combinators are one of the more practical yet challenging applications of monads and combinators. The fact that these concepts are at all possible in Rust demonstrates how far the language has developed towards supporting functional concepts.

Using the lazy evaluation pattern

Lazy evaluation is procrastination, doing work later rather than now. Why is this important? Well, it turns out if you procrastinate long enough, sometimes it turns out that the work never needed to be done after all!

Take, for example, a simple expression evaluation:

```
fn main()
{
    2 + 3;

    || 2 + 3;
}
```

In a strict interpretation, the first expression will perform an arithmetic calculation. The second expression will define an arithmetic calculation but will wait before evaluating it.

This case is so simple that the compiler gives a warning and might choose to discard the unused constant expression. In more complicated cases, the lazy evaluated case will always perform better when not evaluated. This should be expected because unused lazy expressions do nothing, intentionally.

Iterators are lazy. They don't do anything until you collect or otherwise iterate over them:

```
fn main() {
    let a = (0..10).map(|x| x * x);
    //nothing yet

    for x in a {
        println!("{}", x);
```

```
        }
    //now it ran
}
```

Another data structure that intentionally uses lazy evaluation is the lazy list. A lazy list is very similar to an iterator with the exception that lazy lists can be shared and consumed at different paces independently.

In the parser combinator example, we hid a lazy list inside of the parser state structure. Let's isolate that and see what a pure definition looks like:

```rust
use std::rc::Rc;

#[derive(Clone)]
struct LazyList<A: Clone> {
    buffer: Rc<Vec<A>>,
    index: usize
}

impl<A: Clone> LazyList<A> {
    fn new(buf: Vec<A>) -> LazyList<A> {
        LazyList {
            buffer: Rc::new(buf),
            index: 0
        }
    }
    fn next(&self) -> Option<(LazyList<A>,A)> {
        if self.index < self.buffer.len() {
            let new_item = self.buffer[self.index].clone();
            let new_index = self.index + 1;
            Some((LazyList {
                buffer: Rc::clone(&self.buffer),
                index: new_index
            },new_item))
        } else {
            None
        }
    }
}

fn main()
{
    let ll = LazyList::new(vec![1,2,3]);
    let (ll1,a1) = ll.next().expect("expect 1 item");
    println!("lazy item 1: {}", a1);

    let (ll2,a2) = ll1.next().expect("expect 2 item");
```

```
        println!("lazy item 2: {}", a2);

        let (l13,a3) = l12.next().expect("expect 3 item");
        println!("lazy item 3: {}", a3);

        let (l12,a2) = l11.next().expect("expect 2 item");
        println!("lazy item 2: {}", a2);
    }
```

Here, we can see that a lazy list is much like an iterator. In fact, a lazy list could implement the `Iterator` trait; then it really would be an iterator. However, iterators are not lazy lists. Lazy lists inherently have an unlimited capacity to look ahead to any number of items. Iterators, on the other hand, optionally, may implement the `Peekable` trait permitting one look ahead.

There is a fundamental problem at the core of lazy programming, though. Too much procrastination will never complete any task. If you write a program to launch missiles, at some point in the program, it needs to actually launch missiles. This is an irreversible side-effect of running the program. We don't like side-effects, and lazy programming takes an extreme stance against side- effects. At the same time, we need to accomplish the given task though, and that involves making a choice at some point to push the launch button.

Clearly, we can never fully contain the behavior of programs with side-effects. However, we can make them easier to work with. By wrapping side-effects into lazy evaluated expressions, then turning them into monads, what we create are side-effect units. These units can then be manipulated and composed in a more functional style.

The last lazy pattern that we will introduce is **functional reactive programming**, **FRP** for short. There are entire programming languages, such as Elm, based on this concept. Popular web UI frameworks, such as React or Angular, are also influenced by FRP concepts.

The FRP concept is an extension of the side-effect/state monad example. Event handling, state transitions, and side-effects can be turned into units of reactive programming. Let's define a monad to capture this reactive unit concept:

```
    struct ReactiveUnit<St,A,B> {
        state: Arc<Mutex<St>>,
        event_handler: Arc<Fn(&mut St,A) -> B>
    }

    impl<St: 'static,A: 'static,B: 'static> ReactiveUnit<St,A,B> {
        fn new<F>(st: St, f: F) -> ReactiveUnit<St,A,B>
            where F: 'static + Fn(&mut St,A) -> B
        {
```

```
        ReactiveUnit {
            state: Arc::new(Mutex::new(st)),
            event_handler: Arc::new(f)
        }
    }
    fn bind<G,C>(&self, g: G) -> ReactiveUnit<St,A,C>
        where G: 'static + Fn(&mut St,B) -> C {
        let ev = Arc::clone(&self.event_handler);
        ReactiveUnit {
            state: Arc::clone(&self.state),
            event_handler: Arc::new(move |st: &mut St,a| {
                let r = ev(st,a);
                let r = g(st,r);
                r
            })
        }
    }
    fn plus<St2: 'static,C: 'static>(&self, other:
ReactiveUnit<St2,B,C>) ->
ReactiveUnit<(Arc<Mutex<St>>,Arc<Mutex<St2>>),A,C> {
        let ev1 = Arc::clone(&self.event_handler);
        let st1 = Arc::clone(&self.state);
        let ev2 = Arc::clone(&other.event_handler);
        let st2 = Arc::clone(&other.state);
        ReactiveUnit {
            state: Arc::new(Mutex::new((st1,st2))),
            event_handler: Arc::new(move |stst: &mut
(Arc<Mutex<St>>,Arc<Mutex<St2>>),a| {
                let mut st1 = stst.0.lock().unwrap();
                let r = ev1(&mut st1, a);
                let mut st2 = stst.1.lock().unwrap();
                let r = ev2(&mut st2, r);
                r
            })
        }
    }
    fn apply(&self, a: A) -> B {
        let mut st = self.state.lock().unwrap();
        (self.event_handler)(&mut st, a)
    }
}
```

Here, we find that a `ReactiveUnit` holds state, can respond to an input, cause side-effects, and return a value. Reactive units can be extended with `bind` or concatenated with `plus`.

Now, let's make a reactive unit. We will focus on web frameworks since those seem to be popular. First, we render a simple HTML page, as follows:

```
let render1 = ReactiveUnit::new((),|(),()| {
    let html = r###"$('body').innerHTML = '
        <header>
            <h3 data-section="1" class="active">Section 1</h3>
            <h3 data-section="2">Section 2</h3>
            <h3 data-section="3">Section 3</h3>
        </header>
        <div>page content</div>
      <footer>Copyright</footer>
    ';"###;
  html.to_string()
});
println!("{}", render1.apply(()));
```

Here, the unit renders a simple page corresponding to `section 1` on a website. The unit will always render a whole page and does not consider any state or input. Let's give the unit more responsibilities by telling it to render different content based on which section is active:

```
let render2 = ReactiveUnit::new((),|(),section: usize| {

    let section_1 = r###"$('body').innerHTML = '
        <header>
            <h3 data-section="1" class="active">Section 1</h3>
            <h3 data-section="2">Section 2</h3>
            <h3 data-section="3">Section 3</h3>
        </header>
        <div>section 1 content</div>
        <footer>Copyright</footer>
      ';"###;

    let section_2 = r###"$('body').innerHTML = '
        <header>
            <h3 data-section="1">Section 1</h3>
            <h3 data-section="2" class="active">Section 2</h3>
            <h3 data-section="3">Section 3</h3>
        </header>
        <div>section 2 content</div>
        <footer>Copyright</footer>
      ';"###;

    let section_3 = r###"$('body').innerHTML = '
        <header>
            <h3 data-section="1">Section 1</h3>
```

```
            <h3 data-section="2">Section 2</h3>
            <h3 data-section="3" class="active">Section 3</h3>
        </header>
        <div>section 3 content</div>
        <footer>Copyright</footer>
    ';"###;

    if section==1 {
        section_1.to_string()
    } else if section==2 {
        section_2.to_string()
    } else if section==3 {
        section_3.to_string()
    } else {
        panic!("unknown section")
    }
});

println!("{}", render2.apply(1));
println!("{}", render2.apply(2));
println!("{}", render2.apply(3));
```

Here, the unit makes use of the parameter to decide what section should be rendered. This is starting to feel more like a UI framework, but we aren't using the state, yet. Let's try using that to address a common web problem—page tearing. When a large portion of HTML is changed on a web page, the browser must recalculate how the page should be displayed. Most modern browsers do this in stages and the result is an ugly mishmash of components being visibly thrown around the page.

To reduce or prevent page tearing, we should only update portions of the page that have changed. Let's use the state variable along with the input parameter to only send updates when a component has changed:

```
let render3header = ReactiveUnit::new(None, |opsec: &mut
Option<usize>,section: usize| {
    let section_1 = r###"$('header').innerHTML = '
        <h3 data-section="1" class="active">Section 1</h3>
        <h3 data-section="2">Section 2</h3>
        <h3 data-section="3">Section 3</h3>
    ';"###;
    let section_2 = r###"$('header').innerHTML = '
        <h3 data-section="1">Section 1</h3>
        <h3 data-section="2" class="active">Section 2</h3>
        <h3 data-section="3">Section 3</h3>
    ';"###;
    let section_3 = r###"$('header').innerHTML = '
```

```
      <h3 data-section="1">Section 1</h3>
      <h3 data-section="2">Section 2</h3>
      <h3 data-section="3" class="active">Section 3</h3>
  ';"###;
  let changed = if section==1 {
      section_1
  } else if section==2 {
      section_2
  } else if section==3 {
      section_3
  } else {
      panic!("invalid section")
  };
  if let Some(sec) = *opsec {
      if sec==section { "" }
      else {
          *opsec = Some(section);
          changed
      }
  } else {
      *opsec = Some(section);
      changed
  }
});
```

Here, we issue commands to conditionally render changes to the header. If the header is already in the correct state, then we do nothing. This code only takes responsibility for the header component. We also need to render changes to page content:

```
let render3content = ReactiveUnit::new(None,|opsec: &mut
Option<usize>,section: usize| {
  let section_1 = r###"$('div#content').innerHTML = '
      section 1 content
  ';"###;
  let section_2 = r###"$('div#content').innerHTML = '
      section 2 content
  ';"###;
  let section_3 = r###"$('div#content').innerHTML = '
      section 3 content
  ';"###;
  let changed = if section==1 {
      section_1
  } else if section==2 {
      section_2
  } else if section==3 {
      section_3
  } else {
```

```
        panic!("invalid section")
    };
    if let Some(sec) = *opsec {
        if sec==section { "" }
        else {
            *opsec = Some(section);
            changed
        }
    } else {
        *opsec = Some(section);
        changed
    }
});
```

Now, we have a component for the header and another component for the content. We should combine these two into a single unit. FRP libraries would probably have a cool neat way of doing this, but we don't; so instead, we just write a little unit to combine them manually:

```
let render3 = ReactiveUnit::new((render3header,render3content),
|(rheader,rcontent),section: usize| {
    let header = rheader.apply(section);
    let content = rcontent.apply(section);
    format!("{}{}", header, content)
});
```

Now, let's test this out:

```
println!("section 1: {}", render3.apply(1));
println!("section 2: {}", render3.apply(2));
println!("section 2: {}", render3.apply(2));
println!("section 3: {}", render3.apply(3));
```

Each `apply` issues appropriate new update commands. The redundant `apply` to render `section 2` again returns no commands, as intended. This is really lazy code; the good kind of lazy.

What would reactive programming be without event handling? Let's handle a couple of signals and events. On top of the page state, let's introduce some database interaction:

```
let database = ("hello world", 5, 2);
let react1 = ReactiveUnit::new((database,render3),
|(database,render),evt:(&str,&str)| {
    match evt {
        ("header button click",n) =>
render.apply(n.parse::<usize>().unwrap()),
        ("text submission",s) => { database.0 = s;
```

```
format!("db.textfield1.set(\"{}\")",s) },
        ("number 1 submission",n) => { database.1 +=
n.parse::<i32>().unwrap();
format!("db.numfield1.set(\"{}\")",database.1) },
        ("number 2 submission",n) => { database.2 +=
n.parse::<i32>().unwrap();
format!("db.numfield2.set(\"{}\")",database.2) },
        _ => "".to_string()
    }
});

println!("react 1: {}", react1.apply(("header button click","2")));
println!("react 1: {}", react1.apply(("header button click","2")));
println!("react 1: {}", react1.apply(("text submission","abc def")));
println!("react 1: {}", react1.apply(("number 1 submission","123")));
println!("react 1: {}", react1.apply(("number 1 submission","234")));
println!("react 1: {}", react1.apply(("number 2 submission","333")));
println!("react 1: {}", react1.apply(("number 2 submission","222")));
```

We define four event types to react to. Responding to page state changes still works as previously defined. Events that should interact with the database issue commands to update the database locally and remotely. A view of the output JavaScript looks like the following:

```
event: ("header button click", "2")
$('header').innerHTML = '
    <h3 data-section="1">Section 1</h3>
    <h3 data-section="2" class="active">Section 2</h3>
    <h3 data-section="3">Section 3</h3>
';$('div#content').innerHTML = '
    section 2 content
';

event: ("header button click", "2")

event: ("text submission", "abc def")
db.textfield1.set("abc def")

event: ("number 1 submission", "123")
db.numfield1.set("128")

event: ("number 1 submission", "234")
db.numfield1.set("362")

event: ("number 2 submission", "333")
db.numfield2.set("335")
```

```
event: ("number 2 submission", "222")
db.numfield2.set("557")
```

This correspondence demonstrates how simple side-effect units can be composed to create complex programmatic behavior. This is all built from an FRP library that is less than 50 lines long. Imagine the potential utility of a few more helper functions.

Summary

In this chapter, we introduced many common functional design patterns. We used a lot of scary words, such as functor, monad, and combinator. You should try to remember these words and their meanings. Other scary words, such as contravariant, you can probably forget unless you want to pursue math.

In an applied context, we learned that functors can hide information to expose simple transformations on data. The monad pattern allows us to turn sequential actions into units of computation. Monads can be used to create iterators that also behave more like lists. Laziness can be used to defer computation. Also, these patterns can often be combined in useful ways, such as FRP, which is gaining popularity as a tool to develop user interfaces and other complex interactive programs.

In the next chapter, we will explore concurrency. We will introduce the Rust concepts of thread/data ownership, shared synchronized data, and message passing. Thread-level concurrency is something that Rust was specifically designed for. If you have worked with threads in other languages, then hopefully the next chapter will be encouraging.

Questions

1. What is a functor?
2. What is a contravariant functor?
3. What is a monad?
4. What are the monad laws?
5. What is a combinator?
6. Why is the `impl` keyword necessary for closure return values?
7. What is lazy evaluation?

8
Implementing Concurrency

Concurrency is the act of doing two things at the same time. On a single-core processor, this means **multitasking**. When multitasking, an operating system will switch between running processes to give each of them a share of time to use the processor. On a multi-core processor, concurrent processes can run simultaneously.

In this chapter, we will look at different models of concurrency. Some of these tools are relevant, others are used more for educational purposes. Here, we recommend and explain the thread model of concurrency. Further, we will explain how functional design patterns can make it easier to develop programs that use concurrency effectively.

Learning outcomes will include the following:

- Recognizing and applying subprocess concurrency appropriately
- Understanding the nix fork concurrency model and its benefits
- Recognizing and applying thread concurrency appropriately
- Understanding Rust primitive `Send` and `Sync` traits
- Recognizing and applying the actor design pattern

Technical requirements

A recent version of Rust is necessary to run the examples provided:

`https://www.rust-lang.org/en-US/install.html`

This chapter's code is also available on GitHub:

`https://github.com/PacktPublishing/Hands-On-Functional-Programming-in-RUST`

Specific installation and build instructions are also included in each chapter's `README.md` file.

Using subprocess concurrency

A subprocess is a command that is started from within another process. As a simple example of this, let's create a parent process with three children. process_a will be the parent. Consider the following code snippet:

```
use std::process::Command;
use std::env::current_exe;

fn main() {
    let path = current_exe()
                .expect("could not find current executable");
    let path = path.with_file_name("process_b");

    let mut children = Vec::new();
    for _ in 0..3 {
        children.push(
            Command::new(path.as_os_str())
                    .spawn()
                    .expect("failed to execute process")
        );
    }
    for mut c in children {
        c.wait()
         .expect("failed to wait on child");
    }
}
```

The child process, process_b, runs a loop and prints its own process ID. This is shown as follows:

```
use std::{thread,time};
use std::process;
fn main() {
    let t = time::Duration::from_millis(1000);
    loop {
        println!("process b #{}", process::id());
        thread::sleep(t);
    }
}
```

If you run `process_a`, then you will see output from the three `process_b` processes:

```
process b #54061
process b #54060
process b #54059
process b #54061
process b #54059
process b #54060
```

If you inspect the process tree starting at `process_a`, then you will find that three `process_b` processes are attached as children, as shown in the following code:

```
$ ps -a | grep process_a
54058 ttys001    0:00.00 process_a
55093 ttys004    0:00.00 grep process_a
$ pstree 54058
54058 process_a
>    54059 process_b
>    54060 process_b
>    54061 process_b
```

The preceding commands to inspect the process tree require a Unix-like Command Prompt. The subprocess module itself, though, is more or less platform-independent.

Subprocess concurrency is useful if you want to run and manage other projects or utilities. A good example of subprocess concurrency done right is the `cron` utility. `cron` accepts a configuration file that specifies different commands to be run, and a schedule of when to run them. `cron` continues to run in the background and at the appropriate time starts each configured process according to schedule.

Subprocess concurrency is not well suited for parallel computation in general. No resources will be shared between parent and child processes when using the `subprocess::Command` interface. Also, information cannot be shared easily between these processes.

Understanding nix fork concurrency

Before threads were introduced as a standard for POSIX operating systems in 1995, the best option available for concurrency was `fork`. On these operating systems, `fork` was a fairly primitive command that allowed programs to create copies of themselves as child processes. The name `fork` comes from the idea of taking one process and splitting it into two.

`fork` is not platform-independent, specifically it is not available on Windows, and we recommend using threads instead. However, for educational purposes, it is helpful to introduce some of the concepts from `fork` because they are also relevant to threaded programming.

The following code is a translation of the preceding `process_a`, `process_b` example to use `fork`:

```
extern crate nix;
use nix::unistd::{fork,ForkResult};
use std::{thread,time};
use std::process;

fn main() {
    let mut children = Vec::new();
    for _ in 0..3 {
        match fork().expect("fork failed") {
            ForkResult::Parent{ child: pid } => { children.push(pid); }
            ForkResult::Child => {
                let t = time::Duration::from_millis(1000);
                loop {
                    println!("child process #{}", process::id());
                    thread::sleep(t);
                }
            }
        }
    }
    let t = time::Duration::from_millis(1000);
    loop {
        println!("parent process #{}", process::id());
        thread::sleep(t);
    }
}
```

In this example, the parent-child relationship is very similar to our first example. We have three children running and one parent managing them.

It should be noted that forked processes share memory initially. Only when either process modifies its memory, will the operating system then perform an operation called **copy-on-write**, duplicating the memory. This behavior is a first step into shared memory between running processes.

To demonstrate copy-on-write, let's allocate 200 MB of memory and fork 500 processes. Without copy-on-write, this would be 100 GB and would crash most personal computers. Consider the following code:

```
extern crate nix;
use nix::unistd::{fork};
use std::{thread,time};

fn main() {
    let mut big_data: Vec<u8> = Vec::with_capacity(200000000);
    big_data.push(1);
    big_data.push(2);
    big_data.push(3);
    //Both sides of the fork, will continue to fork
    //This is called a fork bomb
    for _ in 0..9 {
        fork().expect("fork failed");
    }
    //2^9 = 512

    let t = time::Duration::from_millis(1000);
    loop {
        //copy on write, not on read
        big_data[2];
        thread::sleep(t);
    }
}
```

Many resources from the parent process also remain available and safe to use from the child process. This is very useful for server applications that listen on a socket in the parent process and poll for incoming connections in the child process. This simple trick permits server applications to distribute work across worker processes:

```
extern crate nix;
use nix::unistd::{fork,ForkResult};
use std::{thread,time};
use std::process;
use std::io::prelude::*;
use std::net::TcpListener;

fn serve(listener: TcpListener) -> ! {
    for stream in listener.incoming() {
        let mut buffer = [0; 2048];
        let mut tcp = stream.unwrap();
        tcp.read(&mut buffer).expect("tcp read failed");
        let response = format!("respond from #{}\n", process::id());
        tcp.write(response.as_bytes()).expect("tcp write failed");
```

```
        }
        panic!("unreachable");
    }

    fn main() {
        let listener = TcpListener::bind("127.0.0.1:8888").unwrap();
        let mut children = Vec::new();
        for _ in 0..3 {
            match fork().expect("fork failed") {
                ForkResult::Parent{ child: pid } => { children.push(pid); }
                ForkResult::Child => { serve(listener) }
            }
        }

        let t = time::Duration::from_millis(1000);
        loop {
            thread::sleep(t);
        }
    }
```

In this example, we start listening for connections on port 8888. Then, after forking three times, we start serving responses with our worker process. Sending requests to the server, we can confirm that separate processes are indeed competing to serve requests. Consider the following code:

```
$ curl 'http://localhost:8888/'
respond from #59485
$ curl 'http://localhost:8888/'
respond from #59486
$ curl 'http://localhost:8888/'
respond from #59487
$ curl 'http://localhost:8888/'
respond from #59485
$ curl 'http://localhost:8888/'
respond from #59486
```

All three workers served at least one response. Combining the first strategy of memory sharing with this new concept of built-in load balancing, forked processes effectively solve several common problems where concurrency is desired.

However, the fork concurrency model is very rigid. Both of these tricks require planning the application to strategically fork after resources are allocated. Fork does not help at all after the processes have been split. In POSIX, there have been additional standards created to address this problem. Sending information over channels or sharing memory are a common pattern, much like in Rust. However, none of these solutions have proved as practical as threads.

Threads implicitly permit inter-process messaging and memory sharing. The risk of threads is that sharing messages or memory may not be thread-safe and may lead to memory corruption. Rust is built from the ground up to make threaded programming safer.

Using thread concurrency

Rust threads have the following features:

- Share memory
- Share resources, such as files or sockets
- Tend to be thread-safe
- Support inter-thread messaging
- Are platform-independent

For the preceding reasons, we suggest that Rust threads are better suited to most concurrency use cases than subprocesses. If you want to distribute computation, circumvent a blocking operation, or otherwise utilize concurrency for your application—use threads.

To show the thread pattern, we can re-implement the preceding examples. Here are three children threads:

```
use std::{thread,time};
use std::process;
extern crate thread_id;

fn main() {
    for _ in 0..3 {
        thread::spawn(|| {
            let t = time::Duration::from_millis(1000);
            loop {
                println!("child thread #{}:{}", process::id(),
            thread_id::get());
                thread::sleep(t);
            }
```

```
            });
        }
        let t = time::Duration::from_millis(1000);
        loop {
            println!("parent thread #{}:{}", process::id(),
            thread_id::get());
            thread::sleep(t);
        }
    }
```

Here, we spawn three threads and let them run. We print the process ID, but we must also print the thread ID because threads share the same process ID. Here is the output demonstrating this:

```
parent thread #59804:140735902303104
child thread #59804:123145412530176
child thread #59804:123145410420736
child thread #59804:123145408311296
parent thread #59804:140735902303104
child thread #59804:123145410420736
child thread #59804:123145408311296
```

The next example to port is the 500 processes and shared memory. In a threaded program, sharing might look something like the following code snippet:

```
use std::{thread,time};
use std::sync::{Mutex, Arc};

fn main() {
    let mut big_data: Vec<u8> = Vec::with_capacity(200000000);
    big_data.push(1);
    big_data.push(2);
    big_data.push(3);
    let big_data = Arc::new(Mutex::new(big_data));
    for _ in 0..512 {
        let big_data = Arc::clone(&big_data);
        thread::spawn(move || {
            let t = time::Duration::from_millis(1000);
            loop {
                let d = big_data.lock().unwrap();
                (*d)[2];
                thread::sleep(t);
            }
        });
    }
    let t = time::Duration::from_millis(1000);
    loop {
```

```
        thread::sleep(t);
    }
}
```

The process starts 500 threads, all sharing the same memory. Also, thanks to the lock, we could modify this memory safely if we wanted.

Let's try the server example, as shown in the following code:

```
use std::{thread,time};
use std::process;
extern crate thread_id;
use std::io::prelude::*;
use std::net::{TcpListener,TcpStream};
use std::sync::{Arc,Mutex};

fn serve(incoming: Arc<Mutex<Vec<TcpStream>>>) {
    let t = time::Duration::from_millis(10);
    loop {
        {
            let mut incoming = incoming.lock().unwrap();
            for stream in incoming.iter() {
                let mut buffer = [0; 2048];
                let mut tcp = stream;
                tcp.read(&mut buffer).expect("tcp read failed");
                let response = format!("respond from #{}:{}\n",
                    process::id(), thread_id::get());
                tcp.write(response.as_bytes()).expect("tcp write failed");
            }
            incoming.clear();
        }
        thread::sleep(t);
    }
}

fn main() {
    let listener = TcpListener::bind("127.0.0.1:8888").unwrap();
    let incoming = Vec::new();
    let incoming = Arc::new(Mutex::new(incoming));
    for _ in 0..3 {
        let incoming = Arc::clone(&incoming);
        thread::spawn(move || {
            serve(incoming);
        });
    }

    for stream in listener.incoming() {
        let mut incoming = incoming.lock().unwrap();
```

```
                    (*incoming).push(stream.unwrap());
            }
        }
    }
```

Here, three worker processes scrape a queue of requests that get served down from the parent process. All three children and the parent need to read and mutate the request queue. To mutate the request queue, each thread must lock the data. There is a dance here that the children and parent do to avoid holding the lock for too long. If one thread monopolizes the locked resource, then all other processes wanting to use the data must wait.

The trade-off of locking and waiting is called **contention**. In the worst case scenario, two threads can each hold a lock while waiting for the other thread to release the lock it holds. This is called **deadlock**.

Contention is a difficult problem associated with mutable shared state. For the preceding server case, it would have been better to send messages to children threads. Message passing does not create locks.

Here is a lock-free server:

```
use std::{thread,time};
use std::process;
use std::io::prelude::*;
extern crate thread_id;
use std::net::{TcpListener,TcpStream};
use std::sync::mpsc::{channel,Receiver};
use std::collections::VecDeque;

fn serve(receiver: Receiver<TcpStream>) {
    let t = time::Duration::from_millis(10);
    loop {
        let mut tcp = receiver.recv().unwrap();
        let mut buffer = [0; 2048];
        tcp.read(&mut buffer).expect("tcp read failed");
        let response = format!("respond from #{}:{}\n", process::id(),
            thread_id::get());
        tcp.write(response.as_bytes()).expect("tcp write failed");
        thread::sleep(t);
    }
}

fn main() {
    let listener = TcpListener::bind("127.0.0.1:8888").unwrap();
    let mut channels = VecDeque::new();
    for _ in 0..3 {
```

```
        let (sender, receiver) = channel();
        channels.push_back(sender);
        thread::spawn(move || {
            serve(receiver);
        });
    }
    for stream in listener.incoming() {
        let round_robin = channels.pop_front().unwrap();
        round_robin.send(stream.unwrap()).unwrap();
        channels.push_back(round_robin);
    }
}
```

Channels work much better in this situation. This multi-threaded server has load balancing controlled from the parent process and does not suffer from lock contention.

Channels are not strictly better than shared state. For example, legitimately contentious resources are good to handle with locks. Consider the following code snippet:

```
use std::{thread,time};
extern crate rand;
use std::sync::{Arc,Mutex};
#[macro_use] extern crate lazy_static;
lazy_static! {
    static ref NEURAL_NET_WEIGHTS: Vec<Arc<Mutex<Vec<f64>>>> = {
        let mut nn = Vec::with_capacity(10000);
        for _ in 0..10000 {
            let mut mm = Vec::with_capacity(100);
            for _ in 0..100 {
                mm.push(rand::random::<f64>());
            }
            let mm = Arc::new(Mutex::new(mm));
            nn.push(mm);
        }
        nn
    };
}

fn train() {
    let t = time::Duration::from_millis(100);
    loop {
        for _ in 0..100 {
            let update_position = rand::random::<u64>() % 1000000;
            let update_column = update_position / 10000;
            let update_row = update_position % 100;
            let update_value = rand::random::<f64>();
            let mut update_column = NEURAL_NET_WEIGHTS[update_column as
```

```
      usize].lock().unwrap();
              update_column[update_row as usize] = update_value;
          }
          thread::sleep(t);
      }
  }

  fn main() {
      let t = time::Duration::from_millis(1000);
      for _ in 0..500 {
          thread::spawn(train);
      }
      loop {
          thread::sleep(t);
      }
  }
```

Here, we have a large mutable data structure (a neural network) that is broken into rows and columns. Each column has a thread-safe lock. Row data is all associated with the same lock. This pattern is useful for data and computation-heavy programs. Neural network training is a good example of where this technique may be relevant. Unfortunately, the code does not implement an actual neural network, but it does demonstrate how lock concurrency could be used to do so.

Understanding Send and Sync traits

In the previous neural network example, we used a static data structure that was shared between threads without being wrapped in a counter or lock. It contained locks, but why was the outer data structure permitted to be shared?

To answer this question, let's first review the rules of ownership:

- Each value in Rust has a variable that's called its **owner**
- There can only be one owner at a time
- When the owner goes out of scope, the value will be dropped

With these rules in mind, let's try to share a variable across threads, as follows:

```
      use std::thread;

      fn main() {
          let a = vec![1, 2, 3];

          thread::spawn(|| {
```

```
        println!("a = {:?}", a);
    });
}
```

If we try to compile this, then we will get an error complaining of the following:

closure may outlive the current function, but it borrows `a`, which is owned by the current function

This error indicates the following:

- Referencing variable a from inside the closure is okay
- The closure lives longer than variable a

Closures sent to threads must have a static lifetime. Variable a is a local variable, and thus will go out of scope before the static closure.

To fix this error, it is common to move the variable a into the closure. Thus, a will inherit the same lifetime as the closure:

```
use std::thread;

fn main() {
    let a = vec![1, 2, 3];

    thread::spawn(move || {
        println!("a = {:?}", a);
    });
}
```

This program will compile and run. Ownership of the variable a is transferred to the closure and therefore lifetime issues are avoided. It should be noted that transferring ownership of a variable implies that the original variable is no longer valid. This is caused by ownership rule number 2—there can only by one owner at a time.

If we try to share the variable again, we get an error:

```
use std::thread;

fn main() {
    let a = vec![1, 2, 3];

    thread::spawn(move || {
        println!("a = {:?}", a);
    });
```

```
        thread::spawn(move || {
            println!("a = {:?}", a);
        });
    }
```

Compiling this gives us this error message:

```
$ rustc t.rs
error[E0382]: capture of moved value: `a`
  --> t.rs:11:28
   |
6  |     thread::spawn(move || {
   |                   ------- value moved (into closure) here
...
11 |         println!("a = {:?}", a);
   |                              ^ value captured here after move
   |
   = note: move occurs because `a` has type `std::vec::Vec<i32>`, which
does not implement the `Copy` trait

error: aborting due to previous error

For more information about this error, try `rustc --explain E0382`.
```

This compiler error is a bit complicated. It says the following:

- **Capture of moved value**: a
- Value moved (into closure) here
- Value captured here after move
- Note—move occurs because a does not implement the `Copy` trait

Part four of the error tells us that if a implements the `Copy` trait, then we would not have this error. However, that would be implicitly copying the variable for us, meaning we would not be sharing data. So, that suggestion is not useful for us.

The main problem is part one—capture of moved value a:

1. First we move the variable a into the first closure. We needed to do this to avoid the lifetime problem and to use the variable. Using a variable in a closure is called a **capture**.
2. Next we use variable a in the second closure. This is the `value captured after move`.

So our problem is that moving variable a invalidates it for further use. A much simpler example of this problem would be as follows:

```
fn main() {
    let a = vec![1, 2, 3];
    let b = a;
}
```

By moving ownership of the value in a into b, we invalidate the original variable.

So what do we do? Are we stuck?

In the neural network example, we used a shared data structure, so clearly there must be a way. If there is a way, hopefully there is also a rule to make sense of the problem. To fully understand thread-safety rules in Rust, you must understand three concepts—scope, Send, and Sync.

First, let's address scope. Scope for threads means that variables used must be allowed to capture the variables that they used. Variables can be captured by value, by reference, or by mutable reference.

Our first example, not using move, almost worked. The only problem was that the lifetime of the variable we used went out of scope too soon. All thread closures must have static lifetimes, and therefore variables that they capture must also have static lifetimes. Adjusting for this, we can create a simple two-thread program that captures our variable, A, by reference and therefore does not move the variable:

```
use std::thread;

fn main() {
    static A: [u8; 100] = [22; 100];

    thread::spawn(|| {
        A[3];
    });

    thread::spawn(|| {
        A[3]
    });
}
```

Reading from static variables is safe. Mutating static variables is unsafe. Static variables are also disallowed from allocating heap memory directly, so they can be difficult to work with.

Using the `lazy_static` crate is a good way to create static variables with types that have memory allocation and need initialization:

```
use std::thread;
#[macro_use] extern crate lazy_static;

lazy_static! {
    static ref A: Vec<u32> = {
        vec![1, 2, 3]
    };
}

fn main() {
    thread::spawn(|| {
        A[1];
    });

    thread::spawn(|| {
        A[2];
    });
}
```

A second way to fix scope problems is to use a reference counter, such as `Arc`. Here, we use `Arc` instead of `Rc` because `Arc` is thread-safe and `Rc` is not. Consider the following code:

```
use std::thread;
use std::sync::{Arc};

fn main() {
    let a = Arc::new(vec![1, 2, 3]);
    {
        let a = Arc::clone(&a);
        thread::spawn(move || {
            a[1];
        });
    }

    {
        let a = Arc::clone(&a);
        thread::spawn(move || {
            a[1];
        });
    }
}
```

The reference counter moves the reference into the closure. However, the internal data is shared, so it is then possible to reference common data.

If shared data should be mutated, then a `Mutex` lock can allow thread-safe locking. Another useful lock is the `std::sync::RwLock`. This is shown as follows:

```
use std::thread;
use std::sync::{Arc,Mutex};

fn main() {
    let a = Arc::new(Mutex::new(vec![1, 2, 3]));
    {
        let a = Arc::clone(&a);
        thread::spawn(move || {
            let mut a = a.lock().unwrap();
            (*a)[1] = 2;
        });
    }
    {
        let a = Arc::clone(&a);
        thread::spawn(move || {
            let mut a = a.lock().unwrap();
            (*a)[1] = 3;
        });
    }
}
```

So why is mutation allowed after the lock, but not before? The answer is `Send` and `Sync`.

`Send` and `Sync` are marker traits. A marker trait does not implement any functionality; however, it indicates that a type has some property. These two properties tell the compiler what behavior should be allowed with regards to sharing data between threads.

These are the rules regarding thread data sharing:

- A type is `Send` if it is safe to send it to another thread
- A type is `Sync` if it is safe to share between multiple threads

To make mutable data that can be shared across threads, whatever data type, you use must implement `Sync`. The standard Rust library has some thread-safe concurrency primitives, such as `Mutex`, for this purpose. If you don't like the options available, then you can search for another crate or make something yourself.

To implement `Sync` for a type, just implement the trait with no body:

```
use std::thread;

struct MyBox(u8);
unsafe impl Send for MyBox {}
unsafe impl Sync for MyBox {}

static A: MyBox = MyBox(22);

fn main() {
    thread::spawn(move || {
        A.0
    });
    thread::spawn(move || {
        A.0
    });
}
```

Be warned—incorrectly implementing `Send` or `Sync` can cause undefined behavior. The traits are always unsafe to implement. Thankfully, both of these marker traits are generally derived by the compiler, so you will very rarely need to manually derive them.

With these various rules in mind, we can see how Rust prevents many common threading bugs. Foremost, the ownership system prevents a lot of problems. Then, to allow some inter-thread communication, we find that channels and locks can help to safely implement most concurrency models.

This was a lot of trial and error but, in summary, we learned that `thread`, `move`, `channel`, `Arc`, and `Mutex` will get us through most problems.

Using functional design for concurrency

Concurrency forces the programmer to be more careful about information sharing. This difficulty coincidentally encourages good functional programming practices, such as immutable data and pure functions; when computation is not context-sensitive, it tends to also be thread-safe.

Functional programming sounds great for concurrency, but are there downsides?

In one example of good intentions with bad effects, during development of a functional language called **Haskell**, the development team (https://www.infoq.com/interviews/armstrong-peyton-jones-erlang-haskell) wanted to make programs run faster using concurrency. Due to a unique trait of the Haskell language, it was possible to run all expressions and sub-expressions in new threads. The development team thought this sounded great and tested it out.

The result was that more time was spent spawning new threads than doing any computation. The idea still had merit, but it turned out that implementing concurrency automatically would be difficult. There are many trade-offs in concurrent programming. Letting the programmer make decisions regarding these trade-offs is the current state-of-the-art.

So, from functional programming, what patterns have proven useful?

There are many patterns for concurrent programming, but here we will introduce a few primitives:

- **Actors**: Threads and patterns of behavior
- **Supervisors**: Monitor and manage actors
- **Routers**: Send messages between actors
- **Monads**: Composable units of behavior

First, let's look at actors in the following code:

```
use std::thread;
use std::sync::mpsc::{channel};
use std::time;

fn main() {
    let (pinginsend,pinginrecv) = channel();
    let (pingoutsend,pingoutrecv) = channel();
    let mut ping = 1;
    thread::spawn(move || {
        let t = time::Duration::from_millis(1000);
        loop {
            let n = pinginrecv.recv().unwrap();
            ping += n;
            println!("ping {}", ping);
            thread::sleep(t);
            pingoutsend.send(ping).unwrap();
        }
    });
```

```
let (ponginsend,ponginrecv) = channel();
let (pongoutsend,pongoutrecv) = channel();
let mut pong = 2;
thread::spawn(move || {
    let t = time::Duration::from_millis(1000);
    loop {
        let n = ponginrecv.recv().unwrap();
        pong += n;
        println!("pong {}", pong);
        thread::sleep(t);
        pongoutsend.send(pong).unwrap();
    }
});

let mut d = 3;
loop {
    pinginsend.send(d).unwrap();
    d = pingoutrecv.recv().unwrap();
    ponginsend.send(d).unwrap();
    d = pongoutrecv.recv().unwrap();
}
}
```

Here we have two threads sending messages back and forth. Is this really much different than any of the previous examples?

There is a fairly common saying in functional programming that "*a closure is a poor man's object, and an object is a poor man's closure*".

According to object-oriented programming, objects have a type, fields, and methods. The closures we define hold their own mutable state, like fields of on an object. The ping and pong closures have slightly different types. The behavior inside the closure could be thought of as a single nameless method on the closure object. There are similarities here between object and closure.

However, it would be much nicer to use a normal object. The problem with attempting this is that the thread boundary gets in the way. Threads do not expose methods, only message passing. As a compromise, we could wrap the message passing into the form of methods. This would hide all of the channel management and would make programming with concurrent objects much nicer. We call this pattern the actor model.

An actor is very similar to an OOP object with the additional property that it lives in its own thread. Messages are sent to the actor, the actor processes the messages, and maybe sends out messages of its own. The actor model is like a busy city of people living and working doing different jobs but interacting and exchanging with one another according to their own schedules.

There are crates that attempt to provide elegant concurrent actor behavior, but we won't endorse any specifically. For the time being, please just squint your eyes and continue to pretend that closures are similar to objects.

In the next example, let's wrap these actors into functions so that they can be created more easily:

```
use std::thread;
use std::sync::mpsc::{channel,Sender,Receiver};
use std::time;
extern crate rand;

fn new_ping() -> (Sender<u64>, Receiver<u64>) {
    let (pinginsend,pinginrecv) = channel();
    let (pingoutsend,pingoutrecv) = channel();
    let mut ping = 1;
    thread::spawn(move || {
        let t = time::Duration::from_millis(1000);
        loop {
            let n = pinginrecv.recv().unwrap();
            ping += n;
            println!("ping {}", ping);
            thread::sleep(t);
            pingoutsend.send(ping).unwrap();
        }
    });
    (pinginsend, pingoutrecv)
}

fn new_pong() -> (Sender<u64>, Receiver<u64>) {
    let (ponginsend,ponginrecv) = channel();
    let (pongoutsend,pongoutrecv) = channel();
    let mut pong = 2;
    thread::spawn(move || {
        let t = time::Duration::from_millis(1000);
        loop {
            let n = ponginrecv.recv().unwrap();
            pong += n;
            println!("pong {}", pong);
            thread::sleep(t);
```

```
                    pongoutsend.send(pong).unwrap();
            }
        });
        (ponginsend, pongoutrecv)
    }
```

To run the example, we will create three of each type of actor and store the channels in a vector, as shown in the following code:

```
fn main() {
    let pings = vec![new_ping(), new_ping(), new_ping()];
    let pongs = vec![new_pong(), new_pong(), new_pong()];
    loop {
        let mut d = 3;

        let (ref pingin, ref pingout) = pings[(rand::random::<u64>() % 3)
as usize];
        pingin.send(d).unwrap();
        d = pingout.recv().unwrap();

        let (ref pongin, ref pongout) = pongs[(rand::random::<u64>() % 3)
as usize];
        pongin.send(d).unwrap();
        pongout.recv().unwrap();
    }
}
```

Now, we have actors and a really basic supervisor for each actor group. The supervisor here is just a vector to keep track of communication channels for each actor. A good supervisor should periodically check the health of each actor, kill bad actors, and resupply the stock of good actors.

The last actor-based primitive that we will mention is routing. Routing is the method equivalent of object-oriented programming. OOP method calls were originally called **message passing**. The actor model is very object-oriented and accordingly we still call methods by actually passing messages around. We are still using the poor man's objects (closures), so our routing will probably look like a glorified if statement.

To start our actor router, we will define two data types—addresses and messages. Addresses should define all possible destinations and routing behaviors for messages. Messages should correspond to all possible method calls from all actors. Here is our extended ping pong application:

```
use std::thread;
use std::sync::mpsc::{channel, Sender, Receiver};
use std::time;
```

```
extern crate rand;

enum Address {
    Ping,
    Pong
}

enum Message {
    PingPlus(u64),
    PongPlus(u64),
}
```

Then we define our actors. They now need to match against the new Message type, and outgoing messages should have an Address in addition to a Message. Despite the changes, the code remains very similar to before:

```
fn new_ping() -> (Sender<Message>, Receiver<(Address,Message)>) {
    let (pinginsend,pinginrecv) = channel();
    let (pingoutsend,pingoutrecv) = channel();
    let mut ping = 1;
    thread::spawn(move || {
        let t = time::Duration::from_millis(1000);
        loop {
            let msg = pinginrecv.recv().unwrap();
            match msg {
                Message::PingPlus(n) => { ping += n; },
                _ => panic!("Unexpected message")
            }
            println!("ping {}", ping);
            thread::sleep(t);
            pingoutsend.send((
                Address::Pong,
                Message::PongPlus(ping)
            )).unwrap();
            pingoutsend.send((
                Address::Pong,
                Message::PongPlus(ping)
            )).unwrap();
        }
    });
    (pinginsend, pingoutrecv)
}

fn new_pong() -> (Sender<Message>, Receiver<(Address,Message)>) {
    let (ponginsend,ponginrecv) = channel();
    let (pongoutsend,pongoutrecv) = channel();
    let mut pong = 1;
```

```
    thread::spawn(move || {
        let t = time::Duration::from_millis(1000);
        loop {
            let msg = ponginrecv.recv().unwrap();
            match msg {
                Message::PongPlus(n) => { pong += n; },
                _ => panic!("Unexpected message")
            }
            println!("pong {}", pong);
            thread::sleep(t);
            pongoutsend.send((
                Address::Ping,
                Message::PingPlus(pong)
            )).unwrap();
            pongoutsend.send((
                Address::Ping,
                Message::PingPlus(pong)
            )).unwrap();
        }
    });
    (ponginsend, pongoutrecv)
}
```

Each ping pong process loops to consume one message and send two more across. The last component for the program is initialization and routing:

```
fn main() {
    let pings = vec![new_ping(), new_ping(), new_ping()];
    let pongs = vec![new_pong(), new_pong(), new_pong()];

    //Start the action
    pings[0].0.send(Message::PingPlus(1)).unwrap();

    //This thread will be the router
    //This is a busy wait and otherwise bad code
    //select! would be much better, but it is still experimental
    //https://doc.rust-lang.org/std/macro.select.html
    let t = time::Duration::from_millis(10);
    loop {
        let mut mail = Vec::new();

        for (_,r) in pings.iter() {
            for (addr,msg) in r.try_iter() {
                mail.push((addr,msg));
            }
        }
        for (_,r) in pongs.iter() {
            for (addr,msg) in r.try_iter() {
```

```
                    mail.push((addr,msg));
            }
        }

        for (addr,msg) in mail.into_iter() {
            match addr {
                Address::Ping => {
                    let (ref s,_) = pings[(rand::random::<u32>() as usize) %
pings.len()];
                    s.send(msg).unwrap();
                },
                Address::Pong => {
                    let (ref s,_) = pongs[(rand::random::<u32>() as usize) %
pongs.len()];
                    s.send(msg).unwrap();
                }
            }
        }
        thread::sleep(t);
    }
}
```

After initializing the different actors, the main thread starts acting as the router. The router is a single thread with the sole responsibility of finding destinations, then moving, copying, cloning, and otherwise distributing messages to the recipient threads. This is not a complex solution, but it is effective, and uses only the typesafe, thread-safe, platform-independent primitives that we have introduced so far.

In a more complex example, the routing Address will typically have the following:

- An actor role
- A method name
- Argument type signatures

The message would then be the arguments according to the preceding type signature. Sending a message from an actor is as simple as sending your (Address,Message) to the router. The router at this time should be regularly checking each channel for new routing requests. When it sees the new message, it will pick an actor that satisfies the Address condition and send the message to that actor's inbox.

Watching the output, each ping pong action doubles the number of messages received. If each thread didn't do so much sleeping, then the program could get out of hand quickly. Messaging noise is one risk of overusing the actor model.

Summary

In this chapter, we introduced the primitives of concurrent computation. Subprocesses, forked processes, and threads are the basic building blocks of all concurrent applications. In Rust threads, there are additional concerns that are introduced by the language to encourage type and thread safety.

In several examples, we built a concurrent web server using fork or threads. Later, while exploring thread behavior, we looked closely at what data can be shared between threads and how information can be sent between threads safely.

In the design pattern section, we introduced the actor design pattern. This popular technique combines some elements of object-oriented programming with other concepts from functional programming. The result is a programming tool designed specifically for complex resilient concurrency.

In the next chapter, we will explore performance, debugging, and metaprogramming. Performance can be hard to measure or compare, but we will try to introduce habits that are strictly good for performance. To help debugging, we will look at proactive and reactive techniques to solve issues. Proactive debugging is a set of techniques, such as proper error handling, that either prevents bugs or makes them easier to document and resolve. Reactive techniques are useful for difficult bugs that don't have an obvious cause. Finally, metaprogramming can do lots of complicated work behind the scenes to make ugly code look nicer.

Questions

1. What is a subprocess?
2. Why is fork called fork?
3. Is fork still useful?
4. When were threads standardized?
5. Why is `move` sometimes needed for thread closures?
6. What is the difference between `Send` and `Sync` traits?
7. Why are we allowed to lock and then mutate `Mutex` without an unsafe block?

Performance, Debugging, and Metaprogramming

9

Writing fast efficient code can be something to be proud of. It also might be a waste of your employer's resources. In the performance section, we will explore how to tell the difference between the two and give best-practices, processes, and guidelines to keep your application slim.

In the debugging section, we offer tips to help find and resolve bugs faster. We also introduce the concept of defensive coding, which describes techniques and habits to prevent or isolate potential issues.

In the metaprogramming section, we explain macros and other features that are similar to macros. Rust has a fairly sophisticated metaprogramming system that allows the user or libraries to extend the language with automatic code generation or custom syntax forms.

In this chapter, we will learn the following:

- Recognizing and applying good performant code practices
- Diagnosing and improving performance bottlenecks
- Recognizing and applying good defensive coding practices
- Diagnosing and resolving software bugs
- Recognizing and applying metaprogramming techniques

Technical requirements

A recent version of Rust is necessary to run the examples provided:

```
https://www.rust-lang.org/en-US/install.html
```

This chapter's code is available on GitHub:

`https://github.com/PacktPublishing/Hands-On-Functional-Programming-in-RUST`

Specific installation and build instructions are also included in each chapter's `README.md` file.

Writing faster code

> *Premature optimization is the root of all evil*

> *– Donald Knuth*

A good software design tends to create faster programs, while a bad software design tends to create slower programs. If you find yourself asking, "W*hy is my program slow?, then first ask yourself, Is my program disorderly?*"

In this section, we describe some performance tips. These are generally good habits when programming in Rust that will coincidentally lead to improved performance. If your program is slow, then first check to see whether you are violating one of these principles.

Compiling with release mode

This is a really simple suggestion that you should know about if you are at all concerned about performance.

- Rust normally compiles in debug mode, which is slow:

  ```
  cargo build
  ```

- Rust optionally compiles in release mode, which is fast:

  ```
  cargo build --release
  ```

- Here is a comparison using debug mode for a toy program:

  ```
  $ time performance_release_mode
  real 0m13.424s
  user 0m13.406s
  sys 0m0.010s
  ```

- The following is the release mode:

```
$ time ./performance_release_mode
real 0m0.316s
user 0m0.309s
sys 0m0.005s
```

Release mode is 98% more efficient with regard to CPU usage for this example.

Doing less work

Faster programs do less. All optimization is a process of searching for work that doesn't need to be done, and then not doing it.

Similarly, the smallest programs fewer resources less. All space optimization is a process of searching for resources that don't need to be used, and then not using them.

For example, don't collect an iterator when you don't need the result, consider the following example:

```
extern crate flame;
use std::fs::File;

fn main() {
    let v: Vec<u64> = vec![2; 1000000];

    flame::start("Iterator .collect");
    let mut _z = vec![];
    for _ in 0..1000 {
        _z = v.iter().map(|x| x*x).collect::<Vec<u64>>();
    }
    flame::end("Iterator .collect");

    flame::start("Iterator iterate");
    for _ in 0..1000 {
        v.iter().map(|x| x * x).for_each(drop);
    }
    flame::end("Iterator iterate");

    flame::dump_html(&mut File::create("flame-
graph.html").unwrap()).unwrap();
}
```

Needlessly collecting the result of the iterator makes the code 27% slower compared to code that just drops the result.

Memory allocation is similar. Well-designed code preferring pure functions and avoiding side-effects will tend to minimize memory usage. In contrast, messy code can lead to old data hanging around. Rust memory safety does not extend to preventing memory leaks. Leaks are considered safe code:

```
use std::mem::forget;

fn main() {
    for _ in 0..10000 {
        let mut a = vec![2; 10000000];
        a[2] = 2;
        forget(a);
    }
}
```

The `forget` function is seldom used. Similarly, memory leaks are permitted but sufficiently discouraged that they are somewhat uncommon. Rust memory management tends to be such that by the time you cause a memory leak you are probably waist-deep in other poor design decisions.

However, unsused memory is not uncommon. If you don't keep track of what variables you are actively using, then old variables will likely remain in scope. This is not the typical definition of a memory leak; however, unused data is a similar waste of resources.

Optimizing the code that needs it – profiling

Don't optimize code that doesn't need to be optimized. It's a waste of your time and probably poor software engineering. Save yourself the trouble and identify performance problems accurately before attempting to optimize the program.

For a code rarely executed, performance is not affected

It is very common that you will initialize some resource and use it multiple times. Optimizing `initialization` of resources may be misdirected. You should consider focusing on improving the work efficiency. This is done as follows:

```
use std::{thread,time};

fn initialization() {
```

```
        let t = time::Duration::from_millis(15000);
        thread::sleep(t);
    }

    fn work() {
        let t = time::Duration::from_millis(15000);
        loop {
            thread::sleep(t);
            println!("Work.");
        }
    }

    fn main() {
        initialization();
        println!("Done initializing, start work.");
        work();
    }
```

Multiples of small numbers are also small numbers

The reverse may also be true. Sometimes the low frequency of work is overwhelmed by frequent and expensive initialization. Knowing which problem you have will let you know where to start looking to improve:

```
    use std::{thread,time};

    fn initialization() -> Vec<i32> {
        let t = time::Duration::from_millis(15000);
        thread::sleep(t);
        println!("Initialize data.");
        vec![1, 2, 3];
    }

    fn work(x: i32) -> i32 {
        let t = time::Duration::from_millis(150);
        thread::sleep(t);
        println!("Work.");
        x * x
    }

    fn main() {
        for _ in 0..10 {
            let data = initialization();
            data.iter().map(|x| work(*x)).for_each(drop);
        }
    }
```

Measuring first, to optimize it

There are a lot of options for profiling. Here are some that we recommend.

The `flame` crate is one option to manually profile an application. Here we create the nested procedures a, b, and c. Each function creates a profiling context corresponding do that method. After running the profiler we will see proportionally how much time was spent for each call to each function.

Starting with function a, this procedure creates a new profiling context, sleeps for one second, then calls b three times:

```
extern crate flame;
use std::fs::File;
use std::{thread,time};

fn a() {
    flame::start("fn a");
    let t = time::Duration::from_millis(1000);
    thread::sleep(t);
    b();
    b();
    b();
    flame::end("fn a");
}
```

Function b is nearly identical to a, and further calls into function c:

```
fn b() {
    flame::start("fn b");
    let t = time::Duration::from_millis(1000);
    thread::sleep(t);
    c();
    c();
    c();
    flame::end("fn b");
}
```

Function c profiles itself and sleeps, but does not call any further nested function:

```
fn c() {
    flame::start("fn c");
    let t = time::Duration::from_millis(1000);
    thread::sleep(t);
    flame::end("fn c");
}
```

The `main` entrypoint sets up the flame graph library and calls a three times, then saves the flamegraph to a file:

```
fn main() {
    flame::start("fn main");
    let t = time::Duration::from_millis(1000);
    thread::sleep(t);
    a();
    a();
    a();
    flame::end("fn main");
    flame::dump_html(&mut File::create("flame-
graph.html").unwrap()).unwrap();
}
```

After running this program, the `flame-graph.html` file will contain a visualization of what program sections took what percentage of resources. The `flame` crate is easy to install, requires some manual code manipulation, but produces a cool-looking graph.

`cargo profiler` is a tool that extends `cargo` to do performance profiling without any code changes. Here is a random program that we will profile:

```
fn a(n: u64) -> u64 {
    if n>0 {
        b(n);
        b(n);
    }
    n * n
}

fn b(n: u64) -> u64 {
    c(n);
    c(n);
    n + 2 / 3
}

fn c(n: u64) -> u64 {
    a(n-1);
    a(n-1);
    vec![1, 2, 3].into_iter().map(|x| x+2).sum()
}

fn main() {
    a(6);
}
```

To profile the application we run the following command:

```
$ cargo profiler callgrind --bin ./target/debug/performance_profiling4 -n
10
```

This will run the program and collect information regarding which functions were most used. This profiler also has another option to profile memory usage. The output will look like the following:

```
Profiling performance_profiling4 with callgrind...

Total Instructions...344,529,557

27,262,872 (7.9%) ???:core::iter::iterator::Iterator
------------------------------------------------------------
22,319,604 (6.5%) ???:<alloc::vec
------------------------------------------------------------
16,627,356 (4.8%) ???:<core::iter
------------------------------------------------------------
13,182,048 (3.8%) ???:<alloc::vec
------------------------------------------------------------
10,785,312 (3.1%) ???:core::iter::iterator::Iterator::fold
------------------------------------------------------------
10,485,720 (3.0%) ???:core::mem
------------------------------------------------------------
8,088,984 (2.3%) ???:alloc::slice::hack
------------------------------------------------------------
7,639,596 (2.2%) ???:core::ptr
------------------------------------------------------------
7,190,208 (2.1%) ???:core::ptr
------------------------------------------------------------
7,190,016 (2.1%) ???:performance_profiling4
```

This clearly shows us that the most time is spent in iterator and vector creation. Running this command may make the program execute much more slowly than normal, but it also saves writing any code before profiling.

Putting the fridge next to the computer

If you take a snack break while coding, then it would be convenient to have a fridge and microwave next to the computer. If you travel to the kitchen for a snack, then it will take a little longer to satisfy your appetite. If your kitchen is empty and you need to make a grocery run, then the break is even further extended. If your grocery store is empty and you need to drive to a farm to harvest vegetables, then your work environment is clearly not designed for snacking purposes.

This strange analogy illustrates the necessary trade-off between time and space. This relation is not quite a physical law for our purposes, but almost. The rule is that traveling, or communicating, over longer distances is directly proportional to time spent. More distance (d) in one direction also means an increase in available space of quadratic (d^2) or cubic (d^3) scale. In other words building the fridge farther away provides more space for a larger fridge.

Bringing this story back to a technical context, here are some latency numbers that every programmer should know (~2012: `https://gist.github.com/jboner/2841832`):

Request	Time
L1 cache reference	0.5 ns
Branch mispredict	5 ns
L2 cache reference	7 ns
Mutex lock/unlock	25 ns
Main memory reference	100 ns
Compress 1 Kb with Zippy	3000 ns
Send 1 Kb over 1 Gbps network	10000 ns
Read 4 Kb randomly from SSD	150000 ns
Read 1 Mb sequentially from memory	250000 ns
Round trip within same datacenter	500000 ns
Send packet CA	Netherlands	CA	150000000 ns

Here, we can see in specific numbers that if you want a donut and some coffee then you could eat 300,000,000 donuts from the fridge next to your computer before taking your first bite from a Danish.

Capping the Big O

Big *O* notation is a computer science term used to group functions with respect to how fast they grow as the input value gets larger. This term is most often used with respect to algorithm runtime or space requirement.

When using this term in software engineering, we are usually concerned with one of these four cases:

- Constant
- Logarithmic growth
- Polynomial growth
- Exponential growth

When we are concerned with application performance, it is good to consider the Big O efficiency of the logic you are using. Depending on which of the preceding four cases you are dealing with, the appropriate response to optimization strategies may change.

Constanting no growth

Constant time operations are the indivisible units of runtime performance. In the previous section, we provided a table of common operations and how long each one takes. These are, for our purposes as programmers, basically physical constants. You can't optimize the speed of light to make it go faster.

Not all constant time operations are irreducible, however. If you have a procedure that does a fixed number of operations on fixed-size data, then it will be constant time. That does not mean that the procedure is automatically efficient. When trying to optimize constant time procedures, ask yourself these two questions:

- Can any of the work be avoided?
- Is the fridge too far from the computer?

Here is a program consisting of emphasizing constant time operations:

```
fn allocate() -> [u64; 1000] {
    [22; 1000]
}

fn flop(x: f64, y: f64) -> f64 {
    x * y
}

fn lookup(x: &[u64; 1000]) -> u64 {
    x[234] * x[345]
}

fn main() {
    let mut data = allocate();
```

```
    for _ in 0..1000 {
        //constant size memory allocation
        data = allocate();
    }

    for _ in 0..1000000 {
        //reference data
        lookup(&data);
    }

    for _ in 0..1000000 {
        //floating point operation
        flop(2.0, 3.0);
    }
}
```

Then, let's profile this program:

```
Profiling performance_constant with callgrind...

Total Instructions...896,049,080

217,133,740 (24.2%) ???:_platform_memmove$VARIANT$Haswell
-----------------------------------------------------------
108,054,000 (12.1%) ???:core::ptr
-----------------------------------------------------------
102,051,069 (11.4%) ???:core::iter::range
-----------------------------------------------------------
76,038,000 (8.5%) ???:<i32
-----------------------------------------------------------
56,028,000 (6.3%) ???:core::ptr
-----------------------------------------------------------
46,023,000 (5.1%) ???:core::iter::range::ptr_try_from_impls
-----------------------------------------------------------
45,027,072 (5.0%) ???:performance_constant
-----------------------------------------------------------
44,022,000 (4.9%) ???:core::ptr
-----------------------------------------------------------
40,020,000 (4.5%) ???:core::mem
-----------------------------------------------------------
30,015,045 (3.3%) ???:core::cmp::impls
```

We see that the heavy memory allocation is fairly expensive. As for the memory access and floating point calculation, it is seemingly overwhelmed by the expense of the loop that executes them multiple times. Unless there is a clear culprit for poor performance in a constant time procedure, then optimizing this code may not be straightforward.

Logarithmic growth

Logarithmic algorithms are the pride of computer science. If your $O(n)$ for $n=5$ code could have been written with an $O(log\ n)$ algorithm, then surely at least one person will point this out.

A binary search is $O(log\ n)$. A sort is typically $O(n\ log\ n)$. Everything with a log in it is better. This fondness is not misplaced. Logarithmic growth has an amazing property—growth slows down as the input value increases.

Here is a program emphasizing logarithmic growth. We initialize a vector with random numbers having size of 1000 or 10000. Then we use the builtin library to sort and perform 100 binary search operations. First let's capture the time for sort and search for the 1000 case:

```
extern crate rand;
extern crate flame;
use std::fs::File;

fn main() {
    let mut data = vec![0; 1000];
    for di in 0..data.len() {
        data[di] = rand::random::<u64>();
    }

    flame::start("sort n=1000");
    data.sort();
    flame::end("sort n=1000");

    flame::start("binary search n=1000 100 times");
    for _ in 0..100 {
        let c = rand::random::<u64>();
        data.binary_search(&c).ok();
    }
    flame::end("binary search n=1000 100 times");
```

Now we profile the 10000 case:

```
    let mut data = vec![0; 10000];
    for di in 0..data.len() {
        data[di] = rand::random::<u64>();
    }

    flame::start("sort n=10000");
    data.sort();
    flame::end("sort n=10000");
```

```
flame::start("binary search n=10000 100 times");
for _ in 0..100 {
    let c = rand::random::<u64>();
    data.binary_search(&c).ok();
}
flame::end("binary search n=10000 100 times");

flame::dump_html(&mut File::create("flame-
graph.html").unwrap()).unwrap();
}
```

After running this and examining the flamegraphs, we can see that sorting for a vector that is 10 times larger takes barely 10 times as much time—O(n log n). Search performance is hardly affected at all—O(log n). So for practical uses, logarithmic growth is almost negligible.

When trying to optimize logarithmic code, follow the same approach as for constant time optimization. Logarithmic complexity is usually not a good target for optimization, particularly considering that logarithmic complexity is a strong indicator of good algorithm design.

Polynomial growth

Most algorithms are polynomial.

If you have one `for` loop, then your complexity is $O(n)$. This is shown in the following code:

```
fn main() {
    for _ in 0..1000 {
        //O(n)
        //n = 1000
    }
}
```

If you have two `for` loops, then your complexity is $O(n^2)$:

```
fn main() {
    for _ in 0..1000 {
        for _ in 0..1000 {
            //O(n^2)
            //n = 1000
        }
    }
}
```

Higher polynomials are somewhat less common. Sometimes code accidentally becomes a higher polynomial, which you should be careful about; otherwise, let's just consider both the previous cases.

Linear complexity is very common. Any time you process the entirety of data in a collection, the complexity will be linear. The running time of a linear algorithm will be approximately the number of items (n) processed, multiplied by the time to process individual items (c). If you want to make a linear algorithm go faster, you need to:

- Reduce the number of items processed (n)
- Reduce the constant time associated with processing an item (c)

If the time to process an item is not constant or approximately constant, then your overall time complexity is now recursively dependent on that processing time. This is shown with the following code:

```
fn a(n: u64) {
    //Is this O(n)?
    for _ in 0..n {
        b(n)
    }
}

fn b(n: u64) {
    //Is this O(n)?
    for _ in 0..n {
        c(n)
    }
}

fn c(n: u64) {
    //This is O(n)
    for _ in 0..n {
        let _ = 1 + 1;
    }
}

fn main() {
    //What time complexity is this?
    a(1000)
}
```

Higher polynomial complexity is also common but may indicate that your algorithm is poorly designed. In the preceding description, we mentioned that the linear processing time can become dependent on the time to process individual items. If your program is designed carelessly, then it is very easy to string together three or four linear algorithms and unintentionally create an $O(n^4)$ monster.

Higher polynomials are proportionally slower. In the case of algorithms that naively require high polynomial calculations, it is often the case that the algorithm can be pruned to remove calculations that are redundant or entirely unnecessary. Consider the following code:

```
extern crate rusty_machine;
use rusty_machine::linalg::{Matrix,Vector};
use rusty_machine::learning::gp::{GaussianProcess,ConstMean};
use rusty_machine::learning::toolkit::kernel;
use rusty_machine::learning::SupModel;

fn main() {
    let inputs = Matrix::new(3,3,vec![1.1,1.2,1.3,2.1,2.2,2.3,3.1,3.2,3.3]);
    let targets = Vector::new(vec![0.1,0.8,0.3]);
    let test_inputs = Matrix::new(2,3, vec![1.2,1.3,1.4,2.2,2.3,2.4]);
    let ker = kernel::SquaredExp::new(2., 1.);
    let zero_mean = ConstMean::default();
    let mut gp = GaussianProcess::new(ker, zero_mean, 0.5);

    gp.train(&inputs, &targets).unwrap();
    let _ = gp.predict(&test_inputs).unwrap();
}
```

When you need to use higher polynomial algorithms, use a library! This stuff gets complicated fast and improving these algorithms is the main job of academic Computer Scientists. If you are performance-tuning a common algorithm and not expecting to publish your results, then you may likely be duplicating work.

Exponential growth

Exponential performance in engineering is almost always a bug or a dead end. This is the wall that separates algorithms that we use from algorithms that we would like to use but can't due to performance reasons.

Exponential growth in programs is often accompanied by the term `bomb`:

```
fn bomb(n: u64) -> u64 {
    if n > 0 {
        bomb(n-1);
        bomb(n-1);
    }
    n
}

fn main() {
    bomb(1000);
}
```

This program is only $O(2^n)$ and therefore barely even exponential!

Referencing data is faster

There is a rule of thumb that referencing data is faster than copying data. Similarly, copying data is faster than cloning. This is not always true, but it is a good rule to consider when trying to improve program performance.

Here is a function that alternatively uses data by reference, copied, intrinsic cloned, or custom cloned:

```
extern crate flame;
use std::fs::File;

fn byref(n: u64, data: &[u64; 1024]) {
    if n>0 {
        byref(n-1, data);
        byref(n-1, data);
    }
}

fn bycopy(n: u64, data: [u64; 1024]) {
    if n>0 {
        bycopy(n-1, data);
        bycopy(n-1, data);
    }
}

struct DataClonable([u64; 1024]);
impl Clone for DataClonable {
    fn clone(&self) -> Self {
```

```
        let mut newdata = [0; 1024];
        for i in 0..1024 {
            newdata[i] = self.0[i];
        }
        DataClonable(newdata)
    }
}

fn byclone<T: Clone>(n: u64, data: T) {
    if n>0 {
        byclone(n-1, data.clone());
        byclone(n-1, data.clone());
    }
}
```

Here we declare array of `1024` elements. Then using the flamegraph profiling library we apply the above functions to measure the differences between reference, copy and clone performance:

```
fn main() {
    let data = [0; 1024];
    flame::start("by reference");
    byref(15, &data);
    flame::end("by reference");

    let data = [0; 1024];
    flame::start("by copy");
    bycopy(15, data);
    flame::end("by copy");

    let data = [0; 1024];
    flame::start("by clone");
    byclone(15, data);
    flame::end("by clone");

    let data = DataClonable([0; 1024]);
    flame::start("by clone (with extras)");
    //2^4 instead of 2^15!!!!
    byclone(4, data);
    flame::end("by clone (with extras)");

    flame::dump_html(&mut File::create("flame-
graph.html").unwrap()).unwrap();
}
```

Looking at the runtime of this application, we see that the referenced data uses only a small sliver of the resources compared to copying or cloning this data. The default clone and copy traits unsurprisingly give a similar performance. The custom clone is really slow. It does semantically the same thing as all the others, but it is not as optimized at a low level.

Preventing bugs with defensive coding

You don't need to fix bugs that never happen. Preventative medicine is good software engineering that will save you time in the long run.

Using Option and Result instead of panic!

In many other languages, exception handling is performed through `try...catch` blocks. Rust does not automatically provide this functionality, instead it encourages the programmer to explicitly localize all error handling.

In many Rust contexts, if you don't want to deal with error handling, you always have the option to use `panic!`. This will immediately end the program and provide a short error message. Don't do this. Panicking is usually just a way of avoiding the responsibility of handling errors.

Instead, use either the `Option` or `Result` types to communicate error or exceptional conditions. `Option` indicates that no value is available. The `None` value of `Option` should indicate that there is no value but that everything is okay and expected.

The `Result` type is used to communicate whether or not there was an error in processing. `Result` types can be used in combination with the ? syntax to propagate errors while avoiding introducing too much extra syntax. The ? operation will return errors from the function, if any, and therefore the function must have a `Result` return type.

Here we create two functions that return `Option` or `Result` to handle exceptional circumstances. Note the use of the try ? syntax when handling `Result` return values. This syntax will pass through `Ok` values or immediately return any `Err` from that function. For this reason, any function using ? must also return a compatible `Result` type:

```
//This function returns an Option if the value is not expected
fn expect_1or2or_other(n: u64) -> Option<u64> {
    match n {
        1|2 => Some(n),
        _ => None
```

```
        }
    }

    //This function returns an Err if the value is not expected
    fn expect_1or2or_error(n: u64) -> Result<u64,()> {
        match n {
            1|2 => Ok(n),
            _ => Err(())
        }
    }

    //This function uses functions that return Option and Return types
    fn mixed_1or2() -> Result<(),()> {
        expect_1or2or_other(1);
        expect_1or2or_other(2);
        expect_1or2or_other(3);

        expect_1or2or_error(1)?;
        expect_1or2or_error(2)?;
        expect_1or2or_error(3).unwrap_or(222);
        Ok(())
    }

    fn main() {
        mixed_1or2().expect("mixed 1 or 2 is OK.");
    }
```

`Result` types are very common when interacting with external resources such as files:

```
    use std::fs::File;
    use std::io::prelude::*;
    use std::io;

    fn lots_of_io() -> io::Result<()> {
        {
            let mut file = File::create("data.txt")?;
            file.write_all(b"data\ndata\ndata")?;
        }

        {
            let mut file = File::open("data.txt")?;
            let mut data = String::new();
            file.read_to_string(&mut data)?;
            println!("{}", data);
        }
        Ok(())
    }
```

```
fn main() {
    lots_of_io().expect("lots of io is OK.");
}
```

Using typesafe interfaces instead of stringly typed interfaces

Enumerations in Rust are less error-prone than using numbers or strings. Whenever possible, write the following code:

```
const MyEnum_A: u32 = 1;
const MyEnum_B: u32 = 2;
const MyEnum_C: u32 = 3;
```

Similarly, you can write a stringly enumeration:

```
"a"
"b"
"c"
```

It is better to use the following enum type:

```
enum MyEnum {
    A,
    B,
    C,
}
```

This way, functions accepting the enumeration will be typesafe:

```
fn foo(n: u64) {} //not all u64 are valid inputs
fn bar(n: &str) {} //not all &str are valid inputs
fn baz(n: MyEnum) {} //all MyEnum are valid
```

Enums also fit naturally with pattern matching for the same reason. Pattern matching against an enumeration does not require a final error case like the integer or string typed case would:

```
match a {
    1 => println!("1 is ok"),
    2 => println!("2 is ok"),
    3 => println!("3 is ok"),
    n => println!("{} was unexpected", n)
}
```

Using the heartbeat pattern for long running processes

When you want to create a long running process, it is nice to be able to recover from program errors that crash or terminate the process. Perhaps the process runs out of stack space or encounters a `panic!` from some code path. For any number of reasons, a process might get terminated and will need to be restarted.

To accommodate this desire, there are many tools that will watch a program for you and restart it if it dies or stops responding to health checks. Here, we recommend a completely self-contained version of this pattern that is based on Rust concurrency.

The goal is to create a parent process that acts as a monitor and oversees one or more workers. The process tree should look something like this:

```
parent
 —– child 1
 —– child 2
 —– child 3
```

When a child dies or stops responding to health checks, the parent should kill or otherwise clean up the process resources, then start a new process to replace it. Here is an example of this behavior, starting with a subprocess that sometimes dies:

```rust
use std::{thread,time,process};

fn main() {
    let life_expectancy = process::id() % 8;
    let t = time::Duration::from_millis(1000);
    for _ in 0..life_expectancy {
        thread::sleep(t);
    }
    println!("process {} dies unexpectedly.", process::id());
}
```

This worker process is highly unreliable and lives no longer than eight seconds. However, if we wrap it with a heartbeat monitor, then we can make it more reliable:

```rust
use std::process::Command;
use std::env::current_exe;
use std::{thread,time};

fn main() {
    //There is an executable called debugging_buggy_worker
    //it crashes a lot but we still want to run it
```

```
    let path = current_exe()
            .expect("could not find current executable");
    let path = path.with_file_name("debugging_buggy_worker");
    let mut children = Vec::new();

    //we start 3 workers
    for _ in 0..3 {
       children.push(
          Command::new(path.as_os_str())
                .spawn()
                .expect("failed to spawn child")
       );
    }

    //those workers will randomly die because they are buggy
    //so after they die, we restart a new process to replace them
    let t = time::Duration::from_millis(1000);
    loop {
       thread::sleep(t);
       for ci in 0..children.len() {
          let is_dead = children[ci].try_wait().expect("failed to
try_wait");
          if let Some(_exit_code) = is_dead {
             children[ci] = Command::new(path.as_os_str())
                                  .spawn()
                                  .expect("failed to spawn child");
             println!("starting a new process from parent.");
          }
       }
    }
}
```

Now, the running processes will get restarted if they die unexpectedly. Optionally, the parent can check the health status of each child process and restart unresponsive workers.

Validating input and output

Preconditions and postconditions are a great way to lock down program behavior and find bugs or invalid states before they get out of hand.

If you use macros to do this, then the preconditions and postconditions can optionally be run only in debug mode, and removed from production code. The built-in debug_assert! macro does this. However, using assertions for return values is not particularly elegant and, if you forget to check a branch with a return statement, then your postcondition won't be checked.

debug_assert! is not a good choice for the validation of anything dependent on external data or otherwise nondeterministic behavior. When you want to check preconditions or postconditions in production code, you should instead use Result or Option values to handle exceptional behavior.

Here are some examples of preconditions and postconditions in Rust:

```
use std::io;

//This function checks the precondition that [n < 100]
fn debug_precondition(n: u64) -> u64 {
    debug_assert!(n < 100);
    n * n
}

//This function checks the postcondition that [return > 10]
fn debug_postcondition(n: u64) -> u64 {
    let r = n * n;
    debug_assert!(r > 10);
    r
}

//this function dynamically checks the precondition [n < 100]
fn runtime_precondition(n: u64) -> Result<u64, ()> {
    if !(n<100) { return Err(()) };
    Ok(n * n)
}

//this function dynamically checks the postcondition [return > 10]
fn runtime_postcondition(n: u64) -> Result<u64, ()> {
    let r = n * n;
    if !(r>10) { return Err(()) };
    Ok(r)
}

//This main function uses all of the functions
//The dynamically validated functions are subjected to user input
fn main() {
    //inward facing code should assert expectations
    debug_precondition(5);
    debug_postcondition(5);

    //outward facing code should handle errors
    let mut s = String::new();
    println!("Please input a positive integer greater or equal to 4:");
    io::stdin().read_line(&mut s).expect("error reading input");
    let i = s.trim().parse::<u64>().expect("error parsing input as
```

```
integer");
    runtime_precondition(i).expect("runtime precondition violated");
    runtime_postcondition(i).expect("runtime postcondition violated");
}
```

Notice that the user input is out of our control. The best option for validating user input is to return an `Error` condition if the input is invalid.

Finding and fixing bugs

Debugging tools are quite platform dependent. Here we will explain `lldb`, which is available, and macOS and other Unix-like systems.

To start debugging, you will need to compile the program with debugging symbols turned on. The normal `cargo debug build` is usually sufficient:

```
cargo build
```

After the program has been compiled, start the debugger:

```
$ sudo rust-lldb target/debug/deps/performance_polynomial3-8048e39c94dd7157
```

Here we reference the `debugs/deps/program_name-GITHASH` copy of the program. This is necessary for now just because of how lldb works.

After running `lldb`, you will see some information scroll past on startup. Then, you should be dropped into a LLDB Command Prompt:

```
(lldb) command source -s 0 '/tmp/rust-lldb-commands.YnRBkV'
Executing commands in '/tmp/rust-lldb-commands.YnRBkV'.
(lldb) command script import
"/Users/andrewjohnson/.rustup/toolchains/nightly-x86_64-apple-
darwin/lib/rustlib/etc/lldb_rust_formatters.py"
(lldb) type summary add --no-value --python-function
lldb_rust_formatters.print_val -x ".*" --category Rust
(lldb) type category enable Rust
(lldb) target create
"target/debug/deps/performance_polynomial3-8048e39c94dd7157"
Current executable set to
'target/debug/deps/performance_polynomial3-8048e39c94dd7157' (x86_64).
(lldb)
```

Now, set a breakpoint. We will set a breakpoint to stop at function a:

```
(lldb) b a
Breakpoint 1: where =
performance_polynomial3-8048e39c94dd7157`performance_polynomial3::a::h0b267
f360bbf8caa + 12 at performance_polynomial3.rs:3, address =
0x000000010000191c
```

Now that our breakpoint is set, run the r command:

```
(lldb) r
Process 99468 launched:
'/Users/andrewjohnson/subarctic.org/subarctic.org/Hands-On-Functional-
Programming-in-
RUST/Chapter09/target/debug/deps/performance_polynomial3-8048e39c94dd7157'
(x86_64)
Process 99468 stopped
* thread #1, queue = 'com.apple.main-thread', stop reason = breakpoint 1.1
  frame #0: 0x000000010000191c
performance_polynomial3-8048e39c94dd7157`performance_polynomial3::a::h0b267
f360bbf8caa(n=1000) at performance_polynomial3.rs:3
   1    fn a(n: u64) {
   2        //Is this O(n);
-> 3        for _ in 0..n {
   4            b(n);
   5        }
   6    }
   7
Target 0: (performance_polynomial3-8048e39c94dd7157) stopped.
```

After stopping at the breakpoint, LLDB will print some context for where the code is stopped at. Now we can inspect the program. Let's print what variables are defined in this function:

```
(lldb) frame variable
(unsigned long) n = 1000
```

We can similarly print any variable in scope:

```
(lldb) p n
(unsigned long) $0 = 1000
```

When we want to continue the program, type c to continue:

```
(lldb) c
Process 99468 resuming
Process 99468 exited with status = 0 (0x00000000)
```

The program exits here because we did not set any more breakpoints. This method of debugging is nice because it allows you to inspect a running program without constantly adding `println!` statements and recompiling. If nothing else works, that is still an option though.

Metaprogramming

Metaprogramming in Rust has two forms—macros and procedural macros. Both of these utilities accept an abstract syntax tree as new input and output symbols to be compiled. Procedural macros are very similar to normal macros but with fewer restrictions on how they work and how they are defined.

Macros defined with the `macro_rules!` syntax are defined recursively by matching the input syntax to produce output. It is crucial to understand that macro matching happens *after* parsing. This means the following:

- Macros must follow certain rules when creating new syntax forms
- The AST is decorated with information regarding each node's grammar category

Macros can match individual tokens, or a macro can match (and capture) an entire grammar category. The Rust grammar categories are as follows:

- `tt`: This is a token tree (which is a token output from the lexer before parsing)
- `ident`: This is an identifier
- `expr`: This is an expression
- `ty`: This is a type
- `stmt`: This is a statement
- `block`: These are the braces containing a block of statements
- `item`: This is a top-level definition such as a function or a struct
- `pat`: This is the match part of a pattern match expression, also called the **left hand side**
- `path`: This is a path such as `std::fs::File`
- `meta`: This is a meta item that goes inside either `#[...]` or `#![...]` syntax forms

Using these patterns we can create macros to match various groups of syntax expressions:

```
//This macro rule matches one token tree "tt"
macro_rules! match_tt {
    ($e: tt) => { println!("match_tt: {}", stringify!($e)) }
}

//This macro rule matches one identifier "ident"
macro_rules! match_ident {
    ($e: ident) => { println!("match_ident: {}", stringify!($e)) }
}

//This macro rule matches one expression "expr"
macro_rules! match_expr {
    ($e: expr) => { println!("match_expr: {}", stringify!($e)) }
}

//This macro rule matches one type "ty"
macro_rules! match_ty {
    ($e: ty) => { println!("match_ty: {}", stringify!($e)) }
}

//This macro rule matches one statement "stmt"
macro_rules! match_stmt {
    ($e: stmt) => { println!("match_stmt: {}", stringify!($e)) }
}

//This macro rule matches one block "block"
macro_rules! match_block {
    ($e: block) => { println!("match_block: {}", stringify!($e)) }
}

//This macro rule matches one item "item"
//items are things like function definitions, struct definitions, ...
macro_rules! match_item {
    ($e: item) => { println!("match_item: {}", stringify!($e)) }
}

//This macro rule matches one pattern "pat"
macro_rules! match_pat {
    ($e: pat) => { println!("match_pat: {}", stringify!($e)) }
}

//This macro rule matches one path "path"
//A path is a canonical named path like std::fs::File
macro_rules! match_path {
    ($e: path) => { println!("match_path: {}", stringify!($e)) }
}
```

```
//This macro rule matches one meta "meta"
//A meta is anything inside of the #[...] or #![...] syntax
macro_rules! match_meta {
    ($e: meta) => { println!("match_meta: {}", stringify!($e)) }
}
```

Then, let's apply the macros to some different input:

```
fn main() {
    match_tt!(a);
    match_tt!(let);
    match_tt!(+);

    match_ident!(a);
    match_ident!(bcd);
    match_ident!(_def);

    match_expr!(1.2);
    match_expr!(bcd);
    match_expr!(1.2 + bcd / "b" - [1, 3, 4] .. vec![1, 2, 3]);

    match_ty!(A);
    match_ty!(B + 'static);
    match_ty!(A<&(B + 'b),&mut (C + 'c)> + 'static);

    match_stmt!(let x = y);
    match_stmt!(());
    match_stmt!(fn f(){});
    match_block!({});
    match_block!({1; 2});
    match_block!({1; 2 + 3});

    match_item!(struct A(u64););
    match_item!(enum B { C, D });
    match_item!(fn C(n: NotAType) -> F<F<F<F<F>>>> { a + b });

    match_pat!(_);
    match_pat!(1);
    match_pat!(A {b, c:D( d@3 )} );

    match_path!(A);
    match_path!(::A);
    match_path!(std::A);
    match_path!(a::<A,_>);

    match_meta!(A);
    match_meta!(Property(B,C));
}
```

As we can see from the example, token trees are, for the most part, not restricted to normal Rust grammar, only to the Rust lexer. The lexer is aware of opening and closing () [] {} bracketed forms. This is why tokens are structured in a token tree rather than a token list. This also means that all tokens inside macro calls will be stored as token trees and not processed any further until the macro is invoked; as long as we create a syntax compatible with Rust token trees, then other syntax innovations should usually be permitted. This rule applies also to the other grammar categories: grammar categories are just a short hand to match certain pattern of tokens that happen to correspond to Rust syntax forms.

Just matching single tokens or grammar categories probably won't be very useful for a macro. To make use of macros in a practical context, we will need to make use of macro grammar sequences and grammar alternatives. A grammar sequence is a request to match more than one token or grammar category in the same rule. A grammar alternative is a separate rule within the same macro that matches a different syntax. Grammar sequences and alternatives can also be combined in the same macro. Additionally, there is a special syntax form to match *many* tokens or grammar categories.

Here are corresponding examples to illustrate these patterns:

```
//this is a grammar sequence
macro_rules! abc {
    (a b c) => { println!("'a b c' is the only correct syntax.") };
}

//this is a grammar alternative
macro_rules! a_or_b {
    (a) => { println!("'a' is one correct syntax.") };
    (b) => { println!("'b' is also correct syntax.") };
}

//this is a grammar of alternative sequences
macro_rules! abc_or_aaa {
    (a b c) => { println!("'a b c' is one correct syntax.") };
    (a a a) => { println!("'a a a' is also correct syntax.") };
}

//this is a grammar sequence matching many of one token
macro_rules! many_a {
    ( $($a:ident)* ) => {{ $( print!("one {} ", stringify!($a)); )*
println!(""); }};
    ( $($a:ident),* ) => {{ $( print!("one {} comma ", stringify!($a)); )*
println!(""); }};
}

fn main() {
```

```
    abc!(a b c);

    a_or_b!(a);
    a_or_b!(b);

    abc_or_aaa!(a b c);
    abc_or_aaa!(a a a);

    many_a!(a a a);
    many_a!(a, a, a);
}
```

If you've paid attention to the generated code for all of these macros, you might have noticed that all production rules have created expressions. Macro input can be tokens, but output must be a contextually well-formed Rust syntax. For this reason, you cannot write `macro_rules!` as shown here:

```
macro_rules! f {
    () => { f!(1) f!(2) f!(3) };
    (1) => { 1 };
    (2) => { + };
    (3) => { 2 };
}

fn main() {
    f!()
}
```

The specific error from the compiler is as follows:

```
error: macro expansion ignores token `f` and any following
--> t.rs:2:19
   |
2  |     () => { f!(1); f!(2); f!(3) };
   |                 ^
   |
note: caused by the macro expansion here; the usage of `f!` is likely
invalid in expression context
--> t.rs:9:4
   |
9  |     f!()
   |     ^^^^

error: aborting due to previous error
```

The key phrase here is `f!`, which is likely invalid in an expression context. Each pattern of `macro_rules!` output must be a well-formed expression. The preceding example will create well-formed Rust syntax in the end, but its intermediate results are fragmented expressions. This awkwardness is one of the several reasons to use procedural macros, which are much like `macro_rules!` but programmed directly in Rust rather than through the special `macro_rules!` syntax.

Procedural macros are programmed in Rust, but are also used to compile Rust programs. How does that work? Procedural macros must be isolated into their own modules and compiled separately; they are basically a compiler plugin.

To start our procedural macro, let's create a new subproject:

1. Make a `procmacro` directory inside the project root
2. Inside the `procmacro` directory, create a `Cargo.toml` file with the following contents:

```
[package]
name = "procmacro"
version = "1.0.0"

[dependencies]
syn = "0.12"
quote = "0.4"

[lib]
proc-macro = true
```

3. Inside the `procmacro` directory, create a `src/lib.rs` file with the following contents:

```
#![feature(proc_macro)]
#![crate_type = "proc-macro"]
extern crate proc_macro;
extern crate syn;
#[macro_use] extern crate quote;
use proc_macro::TokenStream;
#[proc_macro]

pub fn f(input: TokenStream) -> TokenStream {
    assert!(input.is_empty());

    (quote! {
        1 + 2
    }).into()
}
```

```
}
```

This `f!` macro now implements the preceding semantics without any of the complaints. Using the macro looks like the following:

```
#![feature(proc_macro_non_items)]
#![feature(use_extern_macros)]
extern crate procmacro;

fn main() {
    let _ = procmacro::f!();
}
```

The interface of a procedural macro is really simple. There is a `TokenStream` as input and a `TokenStream` as output. The `proc_macro` and `syn` crates also provide utilities to parse tokens or to easily create token streams using the `quote!` macro. To use procedural macros, there is some additional setup and boilerplate, but after getting past these hurdles the interface is fairly straightforward now.

Additionally, there are many more detailed grammar categories available to procedural macros through the `syn` crate. There are 163 categories (https://dtolnay.github.io/syn/syn/#macros) right now! These include the same vague syntax trees from recursive macros, but also very specific syntax forms. These categories correspond to the full Rust grammar, therefore permitting very expressive macro syntax without having to create your own parser.

Let's make a procedural macro that uses some of these syntax categories. First we make a new procedural macro folder, just like preceding `procmacro`; this one we will name `procmacro2`. Now we define the AST that will hold all of the program information if the user input is valid:

```
#![feature(proc_macro)]
#![crate_type = "proc-macro"]
extern crate proc_macro;
#[macro_use] extern crate syn;
#[macro_use] extern crate quote;
use proc_macro::TokenStream;
use syn::{Ident, Type, Expr, WhereClause, TypeSlice, Path};
use syn::synom::Synom;

struct MiscSyntax {
    id: Ident,
    ty: Type,
    expr: Expr,
    where_clause: WhereClause,
```

```
        type_slice: TypeSlice,
        path: Path
    }
```

The `MiscSyntax` struct will contain all information gathered from our macro. That macro and its syntax is what we should define now:

```
impl Synom for MiscSyntax {
    named!(parse -> Self, do_parse!(
        keyword!(where) >>
        keyword!(while) >>
        id: syn!(Ident) >>
        punct!(:) >>
        ty: syn!(Type) >>
        punct!(>>) >>
        expr: syn!(Expr) >>
        punct!(;) >>
        where_clause: syn!(WhereClause) >>
        punct!(;) >>
        type_slice: syn!(TypeSlice) >>
        punct!(;) >>
        path: syn!(Path) >>
        (MiscSyntax { id, ty, expr, where_clause, type_slice, path })
    ));
}
```

The `do_parse!` macro helps simplify the use of the parser combinators from the `syn` crate. The `id: expr >>` syntax corresponds to the monadic bind operation, and `expr >>` syntax is also a form of a monadic bind.

Now we utilize these definitions to parse input, generate output, and expose the macro:

```
#[proc_macro]
pub fn misc_syntax(input: TokenStream) -> TokenStream {
    let m: MiscSyntax = syn::parse(input).expect("expected Miscellaneous
Syntax");
    let MiscSyntax { id, ty, expr, where_clause, type_slice, path } = m;

    (quote! {
        let #id: #ty = #expr;
        println!("variable = {}", #id);
    }).into()
}
```

When using this macro, it really is a bunch of random syntax. This emphasizes how macros are not limited to valid Rust syntax, which looks like the following:

```
#![feature(proc_macro_non_items)]
#![feature(use_extern_macros)]
extern crate procmacro2;

fn main() {
    procmacro2::misc_syntax!(
        where while abcd : u64 >> 1 + 2 * 3;
        where T: 'x + A<B='y+C+D>;
        [M];A::f
    );
}
```

Procedural macros are very powerful and helpful if Rust syntax becomes annoying for your purposes. For specific contexts it is possible to create very semantically dense code using macros that would otherwise require lots of boilerplate and copy-paste coding.

Summary

In this chapter, we introduced many applied and practical considerations for Rust programming. Performance and debugging are certainly not problems that are exclusive to Functional Programming. Here we tried to introduce tips that are generally applicable but also highly compatible with functional programming.

Metaprogramming in Rust may be considered a functional feature by itself. Logic programming and thereby derived functionality are closely associated with functional programming principles. The recursive, context-free nature of macros also lends itself to a functional perspective.

This is also the last chapter in the book. We hope you have enjoyed the book and we welcome any feedback. If you are looking for further reading, you might want to research some of the topics presented in the final three chapters of the book. There is an enormous amount of material available on these subjects and any path taken will surely further improve your understanding of Rust and functional programming.

Questions

1. How is release mode different from debug mode?
2. How long will an empty loop take to run?
3. What is linear time in *Big O* notation?
4. Name a function that grows faster than exponential growth.
5. What is faster, a disk read or a network read?
6. How would you return a `Result` with multiple error conditions?
7. What is a token tree?
8. What is an abstract syntax tree?
9. Why do procedural macros need to be compiled separately?

Assessments

Functional Programming – a Comparison

1. What is a function?

   A function defines a transformation, accepts data, and returns the result of the transformation.

2. What is a functor?

   A functor defines data, accepts a transformation, and returns the result of the transformation.

3. What is a tuple?

   A tuple is a container of a fixed number of miscellaneous values.

4. What control flow expression was designed for use with Enums?

   Pattern matching expressions are a match for Enums, and vice-versa.

5. What is the name for a function with a function as a parameter?

   Functions of functions are called higher-order functions.

6. How many times will `fib` be called in memoized `fib(20)`?

   `fib` will be called 39 times. `fib` will be invoked 21 times.

7. What datatypes can be sent over a channel?

   Sent data must implement `Send`, which is usually derived by the compiler automatically.

8. Why do functions need to be boxed when returned from a function?

   Functions are traits so they do not have a known size at compile time. Therefore, they must either be parameterized or turned into trait objects with something like `Box`.

9. What does the `move` keyword do?

   The `move` keyword transfers ownership of variables to new contexts.

10. How could two variables share ownership of a single variable?

    Indirect references, such as `Rc`, permit sharing references to the same data.

Functional Control Flow

1. What is the ternary operator?

   The if condition is the ternary operator but has the unique Rust syntax of `if a { b } else { c }`.

2. What is another name for unit tests?

   Unit tests are also called **whitebox testing**.

3. What is another name for integration tests?

   Integration tests are also called **blackbox testing**.

4. What is declarative programming?

   Declarative programming avoids implementation details when describing a program.

5. What is imperative programming?

   Imperative programming focuses on implementation details when describing a program.

6. What is defined in the iterator trait?

   The iterator trait is defined by an associated `Item` type, and the required `next` method.

7. In which direction will fold traverse the iterator sequence?

   `fold` will traverse an iterator from left to right, or more specifically, from first to last.

8. What is a dependency graph?

A dependency graph is a directed graph that describes the dependency relationships between nodes. In our case, we use this to describe relationships of the form *x* must happen before *y*.

9. What are the two constructors of `Option`?

`Option` can be created as `Some(x)` or `None`.

Functional Data Structures

1. What is a good library to serialize and deserialize data?

We recommend `serde`.

2. What do the hashtag derive lines in front of the struct declarations in `physics.rs` do?

These are macros that will automatically derive trait implementations for these data structures.

3. Which comes first in parameterized declarations—lifetimes or traits?

Lifetime parameters must come before trait parameters in parameter declarations.

4. In a trait implementation, what is the difference between parameters on the impl, trait, or type?

The `impl<A, ...>` syntax defines what symbols will be parameterized. The `Trait<A, ...>` syntax defines what trait is being implemented. The `Type<A, ...>` syntax defines what type the trait is being implemented for.

5. What is the difference between a trait and a data class?

The term **data class** is not a Rust term. Think of a data class as if it were a trait but without fewer limitations than what Rust might impose.

6. How should you declare that a package has multiple binaries?

   In `Cargo.toml`, list all of the binaries and their entry points:

   ```
   [[bin]]
   name = "binary1"
   path = "binary1.rs"

   [[bin]]
   name = "binary2"
   path = "binary2.rs"
   ```

7. How do you declare a structure field as private?

   Do not declare it as `public`. Fields are `private` by default.

Generics and Polymorphism

1. What is an algebraic data type?

   An algebraic data type is a kind of composite type formed by combining other types.

2. What is polymorphism?

   Polymorphism is the quality of having many forms.

3. What is parametric polymorphism?

   Parametric polymorphism is the quality of having many forms according to a parameter.

4. What is a ground type?

   A ground type is a type that has no parameters, modifiers, or substitutions. For example, `i32` or `String`.

5. What is Universal Function Call syntax?

   Universal Function Call syntax is used to disambiguate functions or methods. It looks like `Foo::f(&b)` instead of `b.f()`.

6. What are the possible type signatures of a trait object?

   A trait object is any signature for a trait that will give it a known size at compile time. Common examples of this are `&Trait` or `Box<Trait>`.

7. What are two ways to obscure type information?

   Trait objects and traits in general hide information. Associated types also reduce the amount of information necessary to interact with code.

8. How is a subtrait declared?

   ```
   trait SuperTrait: SubTrait1 + SubTrait2 {}
   ```

Code Organization and Application Architecture

1. What are four ways of grouping code into modules?

   Our workshop model has four ways of grouping code together: by type, by purpose, by layer, and by convenience.

2. What does FFI stand for?

   FFI stands for Foreign Function Interface.

3. Why are unsafe blocks necessary?

   The `unsafe` syntax in Rust indicates that you want to use superpowers and that you accept the responsibility.

4. Is it ever safe to use unsafe blocks?

   Nothing is safe. There is an ongoing effort by core Rust developers to rewrite standard library code to use fewer unsafe features. Still, depending on how far down you look, there is no absolute safety in any context. For example, the core compiler is just assumed to always be logically consistent with regards to safety checks (hopefully it is).

5. What is the difference between a `libc::c_int` and an `i32`?

   `c_int` is a direct alias—`type c_int = i32;`.

6. Can linked libraries define functions with the same name?

   C++ uses something called name mangling to export symbols with the same name. However, Rust does not currently recognize this format with `extern`.

7. What type of files can be linked into a Rust project?

   Linked libraries can be of the form `name.a`, `name.lib`, `name.so`, `name.dylib`, `name.dll`, or `name.rlib`, each with their own format.

Mutability, Ownership, and Pure Functions

1. What does `Rc` stand for?

   `Rc` stands for Reference Counted.

2. What does `Arc` stand for?

   `Arc` stands for Atomically Reference Counted.

3. What is a weak reference?

   A weak reference is a reference that is not reference counted or otherwise managed.

4. Which superpowers are enabled in unsafe blocks?

   In an unsafe block, you can dereference a raw pointer, call an unsafe function or method, access or modify a mutable static variable, or implement and unsafe trait.

5. When will an object be dropped?

   An object will be dropped when its owner is dropped or goes out of scope.

6. What is the difference between lifetimes and ownership?

   Lifetimes are a compile-time check. Ownership is a compile-time as well as runtime concept. Both concepts describe the tracking of variables, values, and whether and who uses them.

7. How can you be sure that a function is safe?

   In Rust, there is no way to declare the absence of unsafe behavior in functions.

8. What is memory corruption and how would it affect a program?

There are two types of memory corruption—physical memory corruption and software memory corruption. If your physical memory is corrupted, then you need to replace your hardware. Software memory corruption refers to anything the program has done to destroy the semantic structure of its own program. When memory is corrupted, everything goes wrong; this is one of the hardest classes of bugs to diagnose and treat.

Design Patterns

1. What is a functor?

A functor defines data, accepts a function, and returns a transformation of the data.

2. What is a contravariant functor?

A contravariant functor is a functor where the accepted function may produce 0, 1, or many return values. By comparison, functor's accepted functions must return exactly 1 value.

3. What is a monad?

A monad, parameterized by a single type A, is a value that has a trait exposing two operations, usually named `return` and `bind`. `return` is a function that constructs a new monad<A> from a provided A value. `bind` should incorporate new information to produce a related but separate monad<B>.

4. What are the monad laws?

These equivalencies must hold for strict monads. The three horizontal bars means equivalence:

```
_return(v).bind(f) ≡ f(v)

m.bind(_return) ≡ m

m.bind(f).bind(g) ≡ (|x| f(x).bind(g))
```

5. What is a combinator?

   A functional combinator combines functions. A combinator more generator combines things.

6. Why is the impl keyword necessary for closure return values?

   Closures are traits, not types. Therefore they do not have a size known at compile time. `impl` for a return type tells the compiler to parameterize the return type.

7. What is lazy evaluation?

   Lazy evaluation is when computation is delayed until some point in the future. This is compared to eager evaluation, where computation occurs immediately.

Implementing Concurrency

1. What is a subprocess?

   A subprocess is a child process started by a parent process. The child process must remain under the parent process to continue to be called a **subprocess**.

2. Why is fork called fork?

   fork means a split (process), like a fork in the road, or a forked tongue.

3. Is fork still useful?

   Yes! If you have access to it on your system. For example, the heartbeat pattern is much more elegant with fork.

4. When were threads standardized?

   Threads have never been universally standardized. The Posix standard introduced threads in 1995. Notably, Windows provides no standard or guarantees regarding thread behavior. There are similarities, but no standard.

5. Why is move sometimes needed for thread closures?

   Move tells the compiler that it is OK to transfer ownership of captured variables to the closure.

6. What is the difference between `Send` and `Sync` traits?

   `Sync` is a stronger assertion of thread-safety—a type is `Send` if it is safe to send it to another thread. A type is `Sync` if it is safe to share between threads.

7. What are we allowed to lock, then mutate Mutex without an unsafe block?

   The compiler has determined that Mutex is already safe to use and meets certain requirements for safety. That is not to say that bad things can't happen—a Mutex will poison itself if one of its `MutexGuards` (the thing it returns when a lock is obtained) is dropped during a panic. Any future attempts to lock the Mutex will return an `Err` or `panic!`.

Performance, Debugging, and Metaprogramming

1. How is release mode different from debug mode?

   That depends on your Cargo configuration. By default, there are several compiler flags that have different default values in release versus debug mode. One such flag is the opt-level that gets sent to the llvm code generation—the default debug opt-level is 2, and the default release opt-level is 3. These defaults can be changed in `Cargo.toml`.

2. How long will an empty loop take to run?

   Test it out. Otherwise, it is hard to say for sure on every platform. loop will always be an infinite loop. while true should maybe also be an infinite loop, but will generate a warning. `for _ in 0..99999999 {}` will be removed at opt-level 3 but not opt-level 2.

3. What is linear time in Big *O* notation?

   Linear time is $O(n)$ time.

4. Name a function that grows faster than exponential growth.

   Factorial $O(n!)$ grows faster than exponential growth.

5. What is faster, a disk read or a network read?

   Measure it. There are many physical factors to consider here.

6. How would you return a Result with multiple error conditions?

   Rust recommends using enum types to describe multiple error conditions. Being lazy, you could also use the `std::any::Any` type.

7. What is a token tree?

   A token tree is a tree data structure containing tokens. As a result of Rust lexing, (...), [...], and {...} token groups will become their own branches.

8. What is an Abstract Syntax Tree?

   An abstract syntax tree is like a token tree but it has a strict structure such that only well-formed (Rust) code can be represented by it.

9. Why do procedural macros need to be compiled separately?

   Procedural macros are written with normal Rust code. To be used in compilation, procedural macros need to have already been compiled.

Other Books You May Enjoy

If you enjoyed this book, you may be interested in these other books by Packt:

Network Programming with Rust
Abhishek Chanda

ISBN: 978-1-78862-489-3

- Appreciate why networking is important in implementing distributed systems
- Write a non-asynchronous echo server over TCP that talks to a client over a network
- Parse JSON and binary data using parser combinators such as nom
- Write an HTTP client that talks to the server using reqwest
- Modify an existing Rust HTTTP server and add SSL to it
- Master asynchronous programming support in Rust
- Use external packages in a Rust project

Rust High Performance
Iban Eguia Moraza

ISBN: 978-1-78839-948-7

- Master tips and tricks to make your code faster
- Learn how to identify bottlenecks in your Rust applications
- Discover how to profile your Rust software
- Understand the type system to create compile-time optimizations
- Master the borrow checker
- Learn metaprogramming in Rust to avoid boilerplate code
- Discover multithreading and work stealing in Rust
- Understand asynchronous programming in Rust

Leave a review - let other readers know what you think

Please share your thoughts on this book with others by leaving a review on the site that you bought it from. If you purchased the book from Amazon, please leave us an honest review on this book's Amazon page. This is vital so that other potential readers can see and use your unbiased opinion to make purchasing decisions, we can understand what our customers think about our products, and our authors can see your feedback on the title that they have worked with Packt to create. It will only take a few minutes of your time, but is valuable to other potential customers, our authors, and Packt. Thank you!

Index

www.ingramcontent.com/pod-product-compliance
Lightning Source LLC
LaVergne TN
LVHW081519050326
832903LV00025B/1544